PRAISE FOR *JEWS AND WOR* P9-AFJ-623

"Ingenious and thrilling, *Jews and Words* manages to cram more than 5,000 years of prayers, songs, stories, arguments, praises, curses and jokes into the suitcase of a thin, page-turning work of . . . what? History? Anthropology? Literary criticism? Theology? All of these and more. It's a wonderful book."—Jonathan Safran Foer

"*Jews and Words* is thrilling and entertaining, challenging clichés and stereotypes at every page. Its tone is half serious and half humorous, mixing a mastery of its subject with an informal touch. It promises to be very controversial and widely read."—Mario Vargas Llosa

"*Jews and Words* is a wonderful, a great essay. It will resonate not only in the ears of Jews, but also in the mind of any secular intellectual who retains a certain sensitivity for the wealth of words in our book-religions. The line 'Ours is not a bloodline but a textline' is a drum beat for those who hear the special connotations, and for everyone who embraces the eighteenth-century Enlightenment without forgetting those religious motifs that deserve translation without annihilation."
—Jürgen Habermas

"Absolument passionnant."—Bernard-Henri Lévy

"There are many ways to understand and use *Jews and Words*. It is a heart-stirring tribute to the enduring power of our religious writings, a spirited celebration of a certain kind of Jewish genius that has lasted just as long and a gloss on the Tanakh and the Talmud that allows us to approach the old texts from new points of entry. Above all, father and daughter, authentic and committed Zionists whose beliefs are the same as those of the founders of modern Israel, offer us a way of seeing ourselves not as the victims of history but the makers of history. . . . Captivating, troubling and exhilarating—all three of these adjectives apply with equal force to *Jews and Words*, an important and invigorating contemplation of the shared experiences and values that have always defined the Jewish people."—Jonathan Kirsch, *Jewish Journal*

"Distinguished both by the clarity of its authors' arguments and the intellectual panache they display on the page. It's a little book, perhaps, but also an uncommonly delightful and learned one."—*Los Angeles Review of Books*

"Filled with chutzpah, wisdom, humor, and common sense. . . . The authors have added meaningfully and joyfully to the continuum they celebrate."—*Jewish Book World*

"A provocative mixture of scholarship, sly observation and wry writing that often glistens."—Kirkus Reviews

"*Jews and Words* [is] brimming with such unsentimental affection for these texts and the role they've played in the survival of the Jewish people that those with any interest in the subject are likely to find themselves captivated and inspired by the authors' undisguised enthusiasm. . . . A passionate, sophisticated argument for the central role of texts in Jewish survival."—*Shelf Awareness*

"*Jews and Words* is a thought-provoking essay on language, literature and the eternal question of Jewish identity. . . . Filled with fascinating anecdotes and details, not least the etymologies of various words dating back to ancient Hebrew. . . . A stimulating meditation on what it means to be a Jew and what it means to be a reader."—Toby Lichtig, *Wall Street Journal Europe*

"[An] exhilarating essay."—Michael Kerrigan, *The Scotsman*

"[A] fascinating overview of Jewish intellectual traditions from a secular perspective. . . . Readers with any background will find details and stories to engage with, argue with and think about."—Mona Moraru, *Pittsburgh Post-Gazette*

"In this provocative, playful, speculative journey through the rich, centuries-old heritage of Jewish literature, father and daughter Amos Oz and Fania Oz-Salzberger propose a 'textline' rather than a bloodline—a notion of Jewish lineage that is etched not in blood but in words." —Natasha Lahrer, *Jewish Chronicle*

"These two high-powered Jewish intellectuals deploy their full inventory of literary, biblical and historic insights to their review of the vital role of words as a sustaining force in Jewish life. . . . This slim (232 pages), but insight-packed volume deserves a wide reading audience." —*St. Louis Jewish Light*

"*Jews and Words* is a conversation between two people who love each other, informed by a wonderful sense of humor and a passionate yet measured analysis of language, people, and literature. Honesty shines through every paragraph of this terrific work."—Yehuda Bauer

jewsandwords

jewsandwords

AMOS OZ AND FANIA OZ-SALZBERGER

A companion volume to the Posen Library
of Jewish Culture and Civilization

Yale

UNIVERSITY PRESS

New Haven & London

Excerpt from Amos Oz, *The Silence of Heaven,* copyright © 2000 by Princeton University Press. Used with permission.

Excerpt from Amos Oz, *The Same Sea,* published by Chatto and Windus. Reprinted by permission of The Random House Group Limited.

Excerpt from Zelda, "Each Man Has a Name," originally published by Hakibutz Hameuchad in 1978. Used by permission of Sifriat Poalim—Hakibutz Hameuchad Publishers.

Excerpt from Leah Goldberg, *Where's Pluto,* originally published in Hebrew in 1995 by Sifriat Poalim. Used by permission of Sifriat Poalim—Hakibutz Hameuchad Publishers.

Excerpt from Peter Cole (translator, editor, and introduction), *The Dream of the Poem,* © 2007 by Princeton University Press. Reprinted by permission of Princeton University Press.

Yale University Press books may be purchased in quantity for educational, business, or promotional use. For information, please e-mail sales.press@yale.edu (U.S. office) or sales@yaleup.co.uk (U.K. office).

Designed by Sonia Shannon.
Set in Berkeley type by Keystone Typesetting, Inc.
Printed in the United States of America.

The Library of Congress has cataloged the hardcover edition as follows:
Oz, Amos.
Jews and words / Amos Oz and Fania Oz-Salzberger.
    p.   cm.
Includes index.
"A companion volume to the Posen Library of Jewish Culture and Civilization."
ISBN 978-0-300-15647-8 (cloth : alk. paper) 1. Jews—Intellectual life. 2. Jews—Origin. 3. Jews—History. 4. Bible. O.T.—Criticism, interpretation, etc. 5. Hebrew literature—History and criticism. 6. Judaism—History.
I. Oz-Salzberger, Fania. II. Title.
DS113.O98 2012
305.892'4—dc23   2012022077

ISBN 978-0-300-20584-8 (pbk.)

A catalogue record for this book is available from the British Library.

How odd
Of God
To choose
The Jews.
—William Norman Ewer

Not so odd: the Jews chose God.
—Anon.

The Jews chose God and took his law
Or made God up, then legislated.
What did come first we may not know
But eons passed, and they're still at it:
Enlisting reasoning, not awe,
And leaving nothing un-debated.

contents

preface

This book is an essay. It is a nonfiction, speculative, raw, and occasionally playful attempt to say something a bit new on a topic of immense pedigree. We offer you our personal take on one core aspect of Jewish history: the relationship of Jews with words.

The authors are a father and a daughter. One is a writer and literary scholar, the other a historian. We have discussed and disputed topics relevant to this book ever since one of us was about three years old. Nevertheless, our coauthorship warrants some justification.

The best way to account for our teamwork is to spell up front what this essay says. It says that Jewish history and peoplehood form a unique continuum, which is neither ethnic nor political. To be sure, our history includes ethnic and political lineages, but they are not its prime arteries. Instead, the national and cultural genealogy of the Jews has always depended on the intergenerational transmittal of verbal content. It is about faith, of course, but even more effectively it is about texts. Significantly, the texts have long been available in writing. Tellingly, controversy was built into them from the very start. At its best, Jewish reverence has an irreverent edge. At its best, Jewish self-importance is tinged by self-examination, sometimes scathing, sometimes hilarious. While scholarship matters enormously, family matters even more. These two mainstays tend to overlap. Fathers, mothers, teachers. Sons, daughters, students. Text, question, dispute. We don't know about God, but Jewish continuity was always paved with words.

For this very reason, our history excels as a story. Indeed, several histories and numerous stories are intertwined in the annals of the Jews. Many scholars and writers have braved this maze. Here we are offering a joint walk through some of its pathways, entwining the gazes of a novelist and a historian, and adding our own interlocution to its myriad conversing voices.

In this slender volume no attempt was made to run the gamut of Jewish works, even the best known or the most influential. There are numerous texts we have not read. The essayistic genre can deliver dense and panoramic discussions of vast topics, but it is also particularly prone to selective reading, personal bias, and an arrogant grope for generalization. Regardless of such generic faults, we take full responsibility for each of these shortcomings, and for many others the reader may encounter. Here is another thing our book tries to spell out: in Jewish tradition every reader is a proofreader, every student a critic, and every writer, including the Author of the universe, begs a great many questions.

If this set of suggestions is persuasive, then our joint father-and-daughter project might make sense.

acknowledgments

Naturally, the wisdom and advice of many people have flown into this small book, as has excellent criticism. Our first and foremost thanks go to our family: Nily Oz, Eli Salzberger, and Galia Oz gave this manuscript their sharp readings and shrewd comments; Daniel Oz, Dean Salzberger, and Nadav Salzberger took part in many a meaningful, gritty, and deeply enjoyable intergenerational conversation.

Felix Posen came up with the very idea for this project, and both he and his son Daniel offered unfailing friendship, dedication, and good cheer. It may not seem typical of two native Hebrew speakers like ourselves to engage with their own cultural legacies in English, but we feel that this book belongs squarely and intimately with the Posen Library of Jewish Culture and Civilization. Many fine scholars are at work on the Library's ten volumes, and their work has inspired ours. We share the Library's broad vision, which is by no means a narrow agenda, of Jewish history as a complex and multifarious trove of human voices crisscrossed by significant continuums. The wealth of cultural diversity does not trump the presence of unifying principles. Religion is but one of them.

Several colleagues and friends were kind enough to read and critique the manuscript. They saved us from factual mistakes, errors of judgment, and similar mishaps; those still remaining in the book are ours alone. Heartfelt thanks go to Yehuda Bauer, Menachem Brinker, Rachel Elior, Yosef Kaplan, Deborah Owen, Adina Stern, and an anonymous reader for Yale University Press.

Other intellectual debts, usually in the form of unforgettable exchanges or lectures heard over the years, are gratefully acknowledged. Some of the following persons may not know that they inspired this book, but inspire they did: Shlomo Avineri, Haim Be'er, Susannah Heschel, Ora Limor, Anita Shapira, Daniel Statman, Yedidia Stern, Michael Walzer, and A. B. Yehoshua. Several volume editors in the Posen Library sent us relevant materials, and we are grateful again to Ora Limor and Yosef Kaplan, alongside David Roskies and Elisheva Carlebach.

Most of this book was written during Fania Oz-Salzberger's double tenure at the University of Haifa and at Monash University's Australian Centre for Jewish Civilisation, as the Leon Liberman Chair in Modern Israel Studies. Warm thanks go to my ACJC colleagues and Australian friends Lee Liberman, Les Reti, and Ricci Swart. It is likewise a pleasure to thank the Fellows, staff, and students of the University Center for Human Values, Princeton University, for a zesty year of intellectual adventure in 2009–10.

Sarah Miller and Dan Heaton of Yale University Press gave

this book their subtle and perceptive editorial attention, for which we are particularly thankful. Joyce Rappaport and Yael Nakhon-Harel of the Posen Foundation kindly provided further editorial support. Tammy Reznik held the fort at Monash University. At the University of Haifa, Ela Bauer, Lee Maanit, Boaz Gur, and Alon Kol were of great help during various stages of research and writing; Kalanit Kleemer's administrative support was invaluable.

Books consulted during the process of writing appear in our sources lists, which also provides all references to our quotations. However, a handful of Internet sites deserve special mention. Mechon-mamre.org provided us with a useful bilingual Bible. Some of the English renderings from the Babylonian Talmud originate from the Soncino edition translated by L. Miller and edited by Rabbi Dr. Isidore Epstein, available online at come-and-hear.com/talmud/, often touched up by us, while some other Talmudic quotations are newly translated by the present authors. We benefited from the excellent *ma'agar sifrut ha-kodesh*, the online scriptures search engine at the Hebrew University's *Snunit* website, kodesh.snunit .k12.il. Of similar value is the website of the Center for Educational Technology (CET) at cet.org.il, sponsored by the Rothschild Foundation. Helpful too is the Ben-Yehuda Project at benyehuda.org, a volunteer-run e-book collection of public domain Hebrew literature. The Web, as the historian among us keeps trying to persuade the novelist among us, is a labyrinthine library of letters, a mammoth maze of meanings, and thus a very Talmudic space.

While reiterating our sole responsibility for all errors remaining in this book, we are hoping they might be of the sort that invites dispute rather than derision. After benefiting from so many interlocutors, we look forward to new conversations, especially of the critical kind.

ONE

Continuity

In two and thirty most occult and wonderful paths of wisdom did the Lord of Hosts engrave his name: God of the armies of Israel, ever-living God, merciful and gracious, sublime, dwelling on high, who inhabiteth eternity. He created this universe by the three Sepharim—Number, Writing, and Speech. Ten are the numbers, as are the Sephiroth, and twenty-two the letters, these are the Foundation of all things.

JEWISH CONTINUITY HAS always hinged on uttered and written words, on an expanding maze of interpretations, debates, and disagreements, and on a unique human rapport. In synagogue, at school, and most of all in the home, it has always involved two or three generations deep in conversation.

Ours is not a bloodline but a textline. There is a tangible sense in which Abraham and Sarah, Rabban Yohanan, Glikl of Hameln, and the present authors all belong to the same family

1

tree. Such continuity has recently been disputed: there was no such thing as a "Jewish nation," we are told, before modern ideologues deviously dreamed it up. Well, we disagree. Not because we are nationalists. One purpose of this book is to reclaim our ancestry, but another is to explain what kind of ancestry, in our view, is worth the effort of reclaiming.

We are not about stones, clans, or chromosomes. You don't have to be an archeologist, an anthropologist, or a geneticist to trace and substantiate the Jewish continuum. You don't have to be an observant Jew. You don't have to be a Jew. Or, for that matter, an anti-Semite. All you have to be is a reader.

In his wonderful poem "The Jews," the late Israeli poet Yehuda Amichai wrote:

> The Jews are not a historical people
> And not even an archeological people, the Jews
> Are a geological people with rifts
> And collapses and strata and blazing lava.
> Their annals must be measured
> On the scale of a different measurement.

A geological people: this unique metaphor may speak a deep truth about other nations, too. It need not be only about the Jews. But it resonates very powerfully for us when we reflect on Jewish continuity as primarily textual. The "historical," ethnic, genetic Jewish nationhood is a tale of rift and calamity. It is a landscape of geological disaster. Can we claim a biological pedigree dating, say, to Roman-era Galilean Jews? We doubt it. So much blood of both converts and enemies, of emblematic Khazars and Cossacks, might be flowing in our veins. On the other hand, geneticists today seem to tell us that some of our genes have been on the ride with us for a while.

This is interesting. But totally beside our point.

There *is* a lineage. Our annals *can* be gauged, our history told. But our "scale of a different measurement" is made of words. That is what this book is about.

At this early stage we need to say loud and clear what kind of Jews we are. Both of us are secular Jewish Israelis. This self-definition carries several significances. First, we do not believe in God. Second, Hebrew is our mother tongue. Third, our Jewish identity is not faith-powered. We have been reading Hebrew and non-Hebrew Jewish texts all our lives; they are our cultural and intellectual gateways to the world. Yet there is not a religious bone in our bodies. Fourth, we now live in a cultural climate—in the modern and secular part of Israeli society—that increasingly identifies Bible quoting, Talmudic reference, and even a mere interest in the Jewish past, as a politically colored inclination, at best atavistic, at worst nationalist and triumphalist. This current liberal withdrawal from most things Jewish has many reasons, some of them understandable; but it is misguided.

What does secularism mean to Israeli Jews? Evidently more than it means to other modern nonbelievers. From nineteenth-century Haskalah thinkers to latter-day Hebrew authors, Jewish secularity has furnished an ever-growing bookshelf and an ever-expanding space for creative thought. Here is just one nutshell, from an essay titled "The Courage to Be Secular" by Yizhar Smilansky, the great Israeli writer who signed his books with the pseudonym Samech Yizhar:

> Secularism is not permissiveness, nor is it lawless chaos. It does not reject tradition, and it does not turn

its back on culture, its impact and its successes. Such accusations are little more than cheap demagoguery. Secularism is a different understanding of man and the world, a non-religious understanding. Man may very well feel the need, from time to time, to search for God. The nature of that search is unimportant. There are no ready-made answers, or ready-made indulgences, pre-packaged and ready to use. And the answers themselves are traps: give up your freedom in order to gain tranquility. God's name is tranquility. But the tranquility will dissipate and freedom will be wasted. What then?

Self-conscious seculars seek not tranquility but intellectual restlessness, and love questions better than answers. To secular Jews like ourselves, the Hebrew Bible is a magnificent human creation. Solely human. We love it and we question it.

Some modern archeologists tell us that the scriptural Israelite kingdom was an insignificant dwarf in terms of material culture. For example, the biblical portrayal of Solomon's great edifices is a later political fabrication. Other scholars cast doubt on all manner of continuity between ancient Hebrews and present-day Jews. Perhaps this is what Amichai meant when he said we are "not even an archaeological people." But each of these scholarly approaches, whether factually right or wrong, is simply irrelevant for readers like us. Our kind of Bible requires neither divine origin nor material proof, and our claim to it has nothing to do with our chromosomes.

The *Tanach*, the Bible in its original Hebrew, is breathtaking.

Do we "understand" it to the last syllable? Obviously not.

Even proficient speakers of Modern Hebrew probably misconstrue the original meanings of many biblical words, because their role in our vocabulary differs significantly from what they stood for in Ancient Hebrew. Take this exquisite image from Psalms 104:17, "Wherein the birds make their nests, *hassida broshim beiyta.*" To a present-day Israeli ear, these three words mean "the stork makes its home in the cypress trees." Makes you reflect, by the way, on the winsome frugality of Ancient Hebrew, which can often pull off a three-word phrase that requires three times that number in English translation. And how colorful and flavorful is each of the three words, all nouns, brimming with meaning! Anyway, back to our main point. You see, in Israel today storks don't make their homes on cypresses. Storks very rarely nest here anyhow, and when they settle down in their thousands for a night's rest en route to Europe or to Africa, those needle-shaped cypresses are not their obvious choice.

So we must be getting it wrong; either the *hassida* is not a stork, or the *brosh* is not a cypress. Never mind. The phrase is lovely, and we know it is about a tree and a bird, part of a great praise for God's creation, or—if you prefer—for the beauty of nature. Psalm 104 gives its Hebrew reader the broad imagery, the dense and fine-tuned delight that might be compared to the magic of a Walt Whitman poem. We don't know whether it does the same in translation.

The Bible is thus outliving its status as a holy writ. Its splendor as literature transcends both scientific dissection and devotional reading. It moves and excites in ways comparable to the great literary oeuvres, sometimes Homer, sometimes Shakespeare, sometimes Dostoevsky. But its historical leverage is different from that of these opuses. Granted that other great poems may have inaugurated religions, no other work of literature so effectively carved a legal codex, so convincingly laid out a social ethic.

It is also, of course, a book that gave birth to innumerable other books. As though the Bible itself harked and heeded the command it attributes to God, "go forth and multiply." So even if the scientists and critics are right, and ancient Israel erected no palaces and witnessed no miracles, its literary output is both palatial and miraculous. We mean this in a wholly secular sense.

But let us check and balance. We have many loving things to say about Jewish specificities, but this book is emphatically not intended to be a celebration of separatism or superiority. Jewish culture was never impenetrable to non-Jewish inspiration. Even when it snubbed foreign trends, it often quietly endorsed them. To us, Tolstoy is as giant a pillar as Agnon, and Bashevis Singer does not trump Thomas Mann. There is much that we cherish in "gentile" literature and quite a bit that we dislike in Jewish traditions. Many of the scriptures, including the Bible at its most eloquent, flaunt opinions we cannot fathom and set rules we cannot obey. All our books are fallible.

The Jewish model of intergenerational conversation merits close attention.

Ancient Hebrew texts are continually engaged with two crucial pairings: parent and child, teacher and pupil. These pairs are arguably more important, even more important, than woman and man. The word *dor,* generation, appears dozens of times in both Bible and Talmud. Both opuses love recounting chains of generations, harking from the distant past and pointing to the distant future. A great deal is said about the chain's most basic link, the Father and the Son. (Please be patient about mothers and about daughters; they too inhabit this book.) From Adam and Noah to the destruction of the Judean and Israelite kingdoms, the Bible zooms in and out on particular fathers and sons, most of whom belong to meticulously listed genealogies.

This is by no means unique. Many cultures, probably all cultures, possess patrofilial paradigms at the roots of their collective memory, mythology, ethos, and art. There is a universal context to the numerous biblical dramas of fathers and sons. These are the perennial tales of love and hate, loyalty and betrayal, resemblance and dissimilarity, inheritance and disinheritance. Almost all societies have cherished the imperative of intergenerational storytelling. Almost all cultures have gloried the passing of the torch from old to young. It has always been a primary duty of human memory—familial, tribal, and later national.

But there is a Jewish twist to this universal imperative. "No ancient civilization," Mordecai Kaplan writes, "can offer a parallel comparable in intensity with Judaism's insistence upon teaching the young and inculcating in them the traditions and customs of their people." Is such a generalization fair to other ancient civilizations? We do not pretend to know or judge. But we do know that Jewish boys, by no means only the rich and privileged ones, were put in touch with the written word at a staggeringly young age.

Here is one astounding constant of Jewish history since (at least) Mishnaic times: every boy was expected to go to school from the age of three to the age of thirteen. This duty was imposed on male children and their parents, administered and often subsidized by the community. At school, often a tiny one-room, one-teacher, multiage affair, the boys studied Hebrew—not their mother tongue, and not a living language even in Talmudic times—at a level sufficient for both reading and writing. This ten-year study was unconditional, independent of class, pedigree, and means. Some boys surely dropped out prior to becoming a Bar Mitzvah, but few remained illiterate.

The secret was to teach them a great deal in their earliest years, and wisely pamper them with sweets to munch with their first alphabet. Where other cultures left boys in their mothers' care till they were old enough to pull a plough or wave a sword, Jews started acculturating their youngsters to the ancient narrative as soon as the tots could understand words, at two years old, and read them, often at the ripe age of three. Schooling, in short, began soon after weaning.

The Jewish twist also pertained to the vessel in which the ancient narrative was served up to the scions. Early in our history we began to depend on written texts. On books. The great story and its built-in imperatives passed from generation to generation on tablets, papyri, parchments, and paper. Today, as we write this book, the historian among us checks all our references on her iPad, and she cannot resist the sweet reflection that Jewish textuality, indeed all textuality, has come full circle. From tablet to tablet, from scroll to scroll.

This brings us to our second twain, the teacher and student. All bookish cultures are bound to generate them.

Who were our first Teacher and Pupil? Jewish tradition positions Moses as the teacher of all teachers; but neither Aaron nor Joshua, later tagged as Moses' students, behaves like a student. Nor do they become great teachers. We therefore pinpoint the earliest teacher-student couplet with Eli the priest and his pupil Samuel the prophet. Note that Eli's two biological sons turned evil, whereas his spiritual son did exceedingly well. Therein lies a poignant truth: children can become a great disappointment, but a good pupil will seldom let you down.

Teacher and student, rabbi and *talmid,* are the mainstay of postbiblical Jewish literature up to modern times. It was an elective relationship—"make a rabbi for yourself," the Mishnah tellingly instructs—and thus unlike the biological father-and-son pairing in some ways, yet similar in many others. Rabbis were almost invariably venerated, of course, but students were often respected too. In the Talmud, a clever youngster's opinion sometimes prevailed over his master's. Famous rabbi-*talmid* couples, such as Hillel and Yohanan ben Zakai, or Akiva and Meir, demonstrate a deep truth of this relationship: love and admiration are laced with dispute, and so they ought to be. Disagreement, within reason, is the name of the game. A fine student is one who judiciously critiques his teacher, offering a fresh and better interpretation.

Rabbi and pupil were typically not an isolated pair. Students are expected to become teachers, forming sequences of scholarship across many generations. The Mishnaic *locus classicus* goes thus: "And Moses received the Torah from Sinai, and passed it to Joshua, and Joshua to the elders, and elders to prophets, and prophets passed it to the men of the Great Knesset."

This chain, Rachel Elior tells us, does injustice to the Israelite priests and Levites. They were the earliest scribes and teachers of the Torah. A geological rift occurred between their long tradition and the Second Temple sages, who sealed the written canon and forbade further additions to the scriptures, while at the same paving a new high road to the oral Torah. This term encompasses the numerous rabbinical discussions that eventually constituted the Mishnah and Talmud. They were supposed to have begun soon after the written Torah was given on Mount Sinai, but their practice and documentation probably ensued from the sealing of the Bible. A novel conversational model now developed, with free discussions, interpretations, and scholarly adventures to be heaped upon the canonized books. As the centuries passed, these exchanges too were put to parchment.

During the stormy era of the Second Temple a tension field arose between text-bound priests and creative, disputative sages. The sages, Elior says, formed a veritable democracy of debate and interpretation: an all-male democracy indeed, bound to the hierarchy of intellectual brilliance, but open to every Jewish man with a cerebral penchant, regardless of birth and status.

Note the unusual dynamic: not a simple oral-to-written lineage, but very early spoken or sung lore turned into very early written texts, which were subsequently expanded, edited, and finally sanctified, an act which opened a new era of creative conversation, eventually recorded in books. Jewish culture became highly adept in both spoken and written study. But its inbuilt tension between the innovative and the sacrosanct—crisscrossing the oral and the written—has survived to this day.

And so it went, onward to the Mishnah's sages, the *Tannaim,* passing their torch to the Talmud's *Amoraim,* the post-Talmudic *Savoraim,* the *Geonim* who flourished around 700 CE, the late-medieval *Rishonim,* and the early modern *Acharonim.* The latter term means "the last ones," and in early modern time Jewish orthodoxy indeed froze in its intellectual tracks, unable to renovate its own house. But Jewish non-orthodoxy kept the tradition in its own ways, steering its variegated courses between Moses and modernity. Linked together in this modern string of Jewish learning, openly and joyfully interacting with the non-Jewish world, fraught with frictions, plural of minds, this modern continuum incorporates Mendelssohn (the third great Moses after the prophet and Maimonides), Asher Ginzberg (better known as Ahad Ha'am), Gershom Scholem, Franz Rosenzweig, Martin Buber, Emmanuel Levinas, Mordecai Kaplan, Abraham Joshua Heschel, and Yeshayahu Leibowitz. All of these thinkers still belong, by their own lights, to the great chain of Jewish scholarship, mythically and textually launched on Mount Sinai by Moses, the first teacher.

Farther away, no longer part of a self-professed chain, but with some learned rabbi or bookish mother or synagogue canticle still flickering on their biographical horizon, stand Heine and Freud, Marx and the Marx Brothers, Einstein and Arendt, Hermann Cohen and Derrida. We are listing them here not just because they were Jewish—we are not in the business of smug stocktaking—but because it is evident that these thinkers and artists were etched by something intimately and textually Jewish.

There is a third group. The modern "unchained" Jews have an ancestry of individuals who chose to cut themselves loose from the orthodox sequence of rabbinic scholarship, but not before it left some mark on them: Jesus, Josephus, Spinoza. As with our previous two groups, there are many, many more.

If historical scholarship has any say on the matter, then clearly the Mishnaic account of an ancient chain of rabbinical wisdom is flawed and punctured. Much of it is shrouded in myth. We do not know that Moses ever existed, and Joshua, as we have insinuated, sounds not like a great Torah scholar to us, but rather like a regional warlord. Exactly who were the Elders? What do we know about the Great Knesset? What went on in the early phase of the Babylonian exile?

We do not know, and the scholarship we trust does not provide answers; but we do know that earlier than the first millennium BCE, Hebrew-speaking Israelites already held a concept of peoplehood centered on textual memory. This was the *Brit,* partially translatable as "covenant," denoting their allegiance with God since Abraham, and with the oral and written Torah since Moses. Abraham's *Brit* was familial; Moses already shepherded a people, in Hebrew *Am,* seeing itself as descended from the twelve sons of Jacob, renamed Yisrael. Thus Children of Israel. Were Abraham and Moses mere myths? Perhaps. But a conceptual and textual chain exists ever since the earliest Israelites started using the term *Brit.* And at some point, no later than the third century BCE, a constant written tradition was stabilized, never to be extinguished.

Since at least the third century BCE, then, while the Jews walked the agonizing trail of a "geological people with rifts / And collapses and strata and blazing lava," their textual memory ceased to be geological; it no longer proceeded in leaps and bounds, shrouded in myth and guesswork. A library began. It grew. We have it today on our shelves and in our laptops.

The *Tannaim* began as "pairs," five generations of Sanhedrin leaders, two in each generation, partners and disputants. The last and greatest twosome, Hillel and Shammai, were also the staunchest intellectual rivals. Then comes the Mishnah, with its six generations of sages, each led in turn by a biological descendant of Hillel the Elder himself. The Mishnah sets a record in the intrinsic overlap of biological father-son and intellectual teacher-student dynasties. Whether the meek Hillel really sired so many prominent Mishnaic scholars hardly matters. He sired them intellectually; that much is demonstrable, and that is enough.

The two Talmuds, the Jerusalemite with its six scholarly generations and the Babylonian with its eight generations, draw directly on the Mishnah, securing the scholarly continuum, which was by then a written tradition. Over centuries, both Talmudic communities engendered rabbis and pupils, who in turn became rabbis themselves.

Note the persisting duality, a staple of orthodox Jewish learning to this day. Rabbinic study loves twosomes, either peer adversaries (such as Hillel and Shammai) or the teacher-and-student couplet. Sometimes biological father, teacher, and disputative interlocutor are all rolled in one. Imagine the psychological thickets! It was a very masculine world, almost womanless, analytic, competitive, verbal, libidinal.

Intellectual contest was tough. "Hillel the Elder had eighty disciples, thirty of whom were worthy of the Divine Spirit resting upon them, as [it did upon] Moses our Master, thirty of whom were worthy that the sun should stand still for them [as it did for] Joshua the son of Nun, [and the remaining] twenty were ordinary." Those schoolroom shacks were Ivy League, by the lights of their own inhabitants. And rabbinical studies are not for the fainthearted.

Unlike in Socrates' Athens, and some modern halls of learning, you did not have to be a rich kid to hang around the Master. Some of the greatest rabbis themselves were humble craftsmen and laborers. Shammai was a builder, Hillel a lumberjack, Rabbi Yohanan a cobbler, Rabbi Isaac and Rabbi Joshua were blacksmiths, Rabbi Jose a tanner, Resh Lakish guarded orchards, and Rabbi Nehemiah was a potter. This list is currently quoted with some zest in Israel, where public debate is raging on the widespread aversion of the ultra-Orthodox to modern education and professional training.

Some of the stuff that the *Tannaim* and the *Amoraim* busied themselves with is alien or uninteresting to us, but we must grant them this: the Mishnah and the Talmud document the largest intellect-based hierarchies prior to the rise of universities in the West.

The Mishnah itself was very conscious and curious about its own scholarly origins. Its sages asked some excellent historical questions: why did the Mosaic tablets become an oral Torah? How was the oral Torah put in writing again? Why was the early Hebrew alphabet abandoned, and the square Assyrian alphabet adopted to replace it? Rabbi Jose thought that many years after Moses gave the Torah, Ezra provided the script in which the Torah was heretofore written. Another rabbi suggested that the original scroll must have been written in that square Assyrian alphabet, which we lost for our sins and rediscovered in the days of Ezra.

This must have been one of the earliest discussions in the field we call today the history of the book. Tellingly, even the *Tannaim* felt that some historical gaps merit explanation. They felt a great need to fill those black holes with a smooth genealogy of scholarship. We, by contrast, are not committed to a continuum launched by Moses himself. There may have been eras of little schooling in early Israelite history, the early Iron Age, when humans eked their subsistence from agriculture, and cities rose and fell amid rough warfare.

But the Torah hails from the same Iron Age, and it neither recognizes nor condones the option of raising your male child ignorant of the Holy Writ. We have no historical evidence of illiterate Jewish communities in ancient or medieval times. It stands to reason that for more than two and a half millennia Jewish scholars have maintained a genuine chain of learning, which most Jewish men were more or less able to follow through reading. A lineage of literacy.

In our post-Freudian era, the teacher-student and father-son pairings, sometimes overlapping and metaphorically akin, carry great fascination. Think of it this way: Jewish tradition allows and encourages pupil to rise against teacher, disagree with him, and prove him wrong, up to a point. This is a Freudian moment, quite rare in traditional cultures. It is also a key to intellectual innovation, up to a point. We don't know whether the rabbinical Jews could have broached modernity on their own without that mighty push from the outside world. But we do know that they were able to teach the modernizing world a lesson in good disputative education. Also—witness Marx, Freud, and Einstein—something about strong father figures, intergenerational rebellion, and rethinking old truths.

Up to a point, we say, because rebellion had its limits. You could not throw off the whole business of God, faith, and Torah. If you did, you would be chased away. Even if you were as brilliant and beloved as Elisha ben Abuya, the fallen lord of Mishnaic learning who went over to the Romans, your name would be erased from record in punishment for your apostasy. But wait: Elisha's wisdom was too great to obliterate, so he would still be quoted, and still appears in the Talmud, as "The Other." *Acher.*

This brings us to God's several roles in numerous biblical and Talmudic plots. Even nonbelievers cannot ignore the Deity's crucial importance to the story. From single-handed Creator he becomes a potent agent of intervention and change, though never again will he act alone after the appearance of Adam and Eve. Humans always turn the wheels of the plot alongside the Almighty, and often in his absence. In the Bible, and most clearly in the Talmud, God is a Father, but not a father of the Christian cast. He is a parent to all Children of Israel, and in his female diasporic form of *Shekhinah,* the abode of divine presence, he even mothers them a little, but at the same time he is their strict and tasking Teacher. A history of the Jewish God is therefore a history of evolving notions of Fatherhood, from the ancient, all-seeing, often angry Lord of Hosts to the modern, faith-losing orphan's cry into the void of paternal absence.

This will explain our choice to keep the Almighty gendered, and male. Most Israelis are not even aware of the progressive liturgical practices of degendering, dual-gendering, or feminizing God. Our own secular perspective grew from a modern generation of skeptics who abandoned, as we shall see in the case of Agnon, a distinctly fatherly deity. Or else, felt abandoned by him.

When Rabbi Meir asked Elisha ben Abuya to repent, the latter—on horseback, on the Sabbath!—replied that he had heard God's word from "behind the veil": "Come back, naughty children [Jeremiah 3:14]—except for *Acher.*" God the Father and Teacher can forgive many errant sons, but not Elisha, for the enormity of his betrayal matched his former understanding of the divine. God thus left the son who had been closest to him to languish outside heaven's door. He could not even be sent to hell, because he had studied so much Torah.

Thank goodness for brother figures, then. For, as the Babylonian Talmud goes on to tell us, after ben Abuya's death, Rabbi Meir and Rabbi Yohanan somehow turned things around in such a way, that by the time you flip from page 15a to page 15b in Tractate Hagigah, the soul of the sinful sage *Acher* came to rest in peace, presumably in paradise.

Many disputes were perfectly legitimate, and proudly reported. Judaism can hold a great deal of rivalry under its belt—perhaps because at the end of each argumentative session, the sages could go home to wife, children, and hot food on the table. It was a masculine intellectual universe, to be sure, but it was neither celibate nor Spartan.

The word *chutzpah,* by the way, stems from the Talmudic concept of an "impudent court of justice," *beit din chatzuf,* where two laymen pass judgment on financial disputes, even though the sages decreed that three laymen are a minimal quorum for such decisions. Typically enough, the rabbis disagreed on the question of whether the impudent court's rulings are acceptable. Some said yes. *Chutzpah* may be annoying, but it is here to stay.

The Talmud is very beautiful when it carries a big disagreement with dignity. In the enticing story of Akhnai's Oven
—how can we possibly skip this delicious Talmudic morsel?—
God himself tries to intervene in a rabbinical debate, and ends
up defeated. Never mind that this complex story is coiled like
a snake, piled on confusingly, with a sad ending for one of the
rabbis. Its gist is still so very lovely to the modern eye:

> On that day Rabbi Eliezer brought forward every
> imaginable argument, but they did not accept them.
> Said he to them: "If the *Halakha* agrees with me, let
> this carob-tree prove it!" Thereupon the carob-tree
> was torn a hundred cubits out of its place—others af-
> firm, four hundred cubits. "No proof can be brought
> from a carob-tree," they retorted.

The nitpicking dispute itself, perhaps about an oven and
perhaps about a snake, is not the focal point. But it is utterly
enthralling that God decided to intervene, throwing out miracles in support of Rabbi Eliezer ben Horkanos. That a whole
group of rabbis deemed those miracles irrelevant to the dispute, now that is the heart of the matter.

> Again [Eliezer] said to them: "If the *Halakha* agrees
> with me, let the stream of water prove it!" Where-
> upon the stream of water flowed backwards—"No
> proof can be brought from a stream of water," they
> rejoined. Again he urged: "If the *Halakha* agrees with
> me, let the walls of the schoolhouse prove it," where-
> upon the walls inclined to fall. But Rabbi Joshua re-
> buked them, saying: "When scholars are engaged in a
> halakhic dispute, what have ye to interfere?"

Those hapless schoolhouse walls, by the way, remained askew. "Hence they did not fall, in honour of Rabbi Joshua, nor did they resume the upright, in honour of Rabbi Eliezer; and they are still standing thus inclined." We like this little aside because it is revealing on two points: Talmudic-style respect, and Talmudic-style architecture.

Now comes the apex. The Lord himself raises his voice in support of Rabbi Eliezer:

> Again [Eliezer] said to them: "If the *Halakha* agrees with me, let it be proved from Heaven!" Whereupon a Heavenly Voice cried out: "Why do ye dispute with Rabbi Eliezer, seeing that in all matters the *halakha* agrees with him!" But Rabbi Joshua arose and exclaimed [quoting Deuteronomy]: "It is not in the heavens!"

This passage is a seminal moment in Jewish intellectual history. Rabbi Joshua is our Prometheus. The Talmud itself seems to stop in its tracks, speechless.

> What did he mean by this?—Said Rabbi Jeremiah: That the Torah had already been given at Mount Sinai; we pay no attention to a Heavenly Voice, because Thou hast long since written in the Torah at Mount Sinai, [quoting Exodus], "After the majority must one incline."

The Torah is now a human domain. A majority judgment beats the Almighty in a scholarly argument. No less.

If you wonder what God himself thought of all this, the rabbis already asked the question. And answered in the very same chapter:

> Rabbi Nathan met [the immortal prophet] Elijah and asked him: What did the Holy One, Blessed be He, do in that hour?—He laughed [with joy], he replied, saying, "My sons have defeated Me, My sons have defeated me."

If you read only one Talmudic page in your life, make it Baba Mezi'a 59b.

Much of the Talmud is alien to us Israeli-born seculars. It holds vast inaccessible stretches, either because they are in Aramaic, or simply because they seem atavistic, legalistic, or nitpicky. The Bible, by contrast, is full of geographical markers we recognize, natural imagery we adore, and vignettes of human nature we deeply admire. On top of this generic difference, the Talmud is often associated with religious or nationalist extremism. Most secular Israeli Jews—with a few significant exceptions—leave Talmud to the believers and to the ultrabelievers.

But the Talmud—and particularly the episode of Akhnai's Oven—steered a dramatic new road, shifting away from biblical intimacy with divine intervention. As Menachem Brinker tellingly and concisely put it, Akhnai's Oven signals the transition from prophecy to exegesis.

This is an epochal juncture. Gone is the lone prophet with a direct link to the Almighty. Enter the interpreter, in constant conversation with fellow interpreters, applying human intelligence to the sacred texts, now prone to multifarious readings. While Abraham argued with God and Moses reiterated God's words, the Mishnaic and Talmudic rabbis are in the business of unraveling, elucidating, explaining, and counter-explaining God and Abraham and Moses. Prophecy is mystical, but exegesis is human. So human that mystical intrusion can become downright unwelcome.

Jewish bookishness, in earnest, began in the Talmud:

> They said of Rabban Yohanan ben Zakai, that he did not leave [unread] Scripture and Mishnah, Gemarah, Halakhot and Aggadot, Torah subtleties and Scribes' subtleties, inferences a minori ad majus, analogies, calendric computations, gematrias, conversations of the ministering angels, conversations of demons, conversations of palm trees, launderers' parables and fox fables, great matters and small matters . . .

Ben Zakai was one of the Talmud's brightest lights. The savant's omnivorous reading list goes on for a while, but its thrust is clear. Had he lived today, he would have been the type of reader whom Woody Allen referred to as "a man who knocked off *Finnegans Wake* on the roller coaster at Coney Island." Note the eclecticism, too: a latter-day Rabban Yohanan would devour Tolstoy and Toni Morrison with his morning coffee while skimming two news sites on his electronic device and perusing the small print on his breakfast cereal package. We recognize the type. You don't have to be a rabbi (or a Jew) to belong to that club.

But Rabban Yohanan's own explanation for his reading appetite was duly devout. "That I may cause those that love me to inherit substance, and that I may fill their treasuries." This, by the way, is what we call a Talmudic hyperlink, referring informed readers to the praise of wisdom in Proverbs 8:21. There, the speaker is Wisdom herself, who is "better than rubies, and all things desirable are not to be compared unto her" (8:11). What Yohanan performs here is what the Talmud often does to the Bible: transforming Proverbs' concept of wisdom—legal, political, and practical—to a Talmudic sort of wisdom, bookish. Many books. All manner of books.

We are sure you want to know that the "conversations of palm trees" are. So do we, and we are all in good company, for the great commentator Rashi was also at a loss. But other exegetes inform us that if you stand under two palm trees that lean toward each other, and the day is not too windy, you might intercept information passing between them. So the whole world is a text, indeed.

Let us digress and say something about nonverbal components of cultural memory. We cannot tell whether palm trees convey legible meaning, but we do know that traditions are not made only of words. Every culture has imprinted visual, musical, and behavioral glyphs on its members, and Jews are no exception. A cultural vocabulary can include facial expressions, physical poise and gesture, familiar smells and tastes. Jews building houses in the Diaspora were obligated to leave a stone or a patch of wall unpainted, commemorating the destruction of the Temple. This custom made the naked stone into a word, and the house into a book. It would be telling a story as long as it stood. So does, to this day, the Passover Plate, replete with symbolic food, complementing the Haggadah in its colorful wordless statement. But we will not delve deeper here into the nonverbal libraries of the Jews. We have enough words on our hands.

That absorbing love of texts, embodied by Yohanan ben Zakai, became a long and complex relationship between learned Jews and the written word. Of a fellow savant, Jonathan ben Uzziel, it was said, "When he sat and occupied himself with the Torah, every bird that flew above him was immediately burnt." It is not a kindly Saint Francis we meet here, conversing with animals and birds. These rabbis' fiery passion for learning could easily kindle the flame of fanaticism. Or, at least, unsociability. Rabban Yohanan reportedly "during his whole life . . . never uttered profane talk, nor walked four cubits without [studying the] Torah or without tefillin, nor was any man earlier than he in the house of study."

Quite probably, the Talmudists were not nice people. We seldom, if ever, meet them making plain human conversation. Nonetheless, they seem to have been great teachers. And this brings us back to our central theme, the teacher-parent confluence that worked so well for the Jewish textual continuum.

Traditional Christianity keeps biological parent and doctrinal teacher well apart. Your priest cannot be your father except by metaphor. No Christian Hillel the Elder could hope to beget, in the literal sense, some of his best disciples. We personally think that it is nicer to be able to raise a few students of your very own. But let us not idealize: that poverty-stricken rabbi, trying hard to concentrate on his halakhic responsa in a tiny house full of squealing babes, the roof leaking, the *rebbetzen* muttering her just wifely complaints, was that rabbi never ever a tad jealous of the rotund clergyman in his quiet presbytery up the street?

Nu, as they said in Yiddish roundabouts where our family came from, *azoy*.

In both Bible and Talmud, the Hebrew noun for "son,"

ben, and the verb for "teach," *lamed*, tend to appear in the same sentence. "Parent" of both genders, *horeh*, and "teacher," *moreh*, derive from the same grammatical root. We have already seen that Talmudic rabbi and father often overlap. Jose ben Honi once had a lovely, albeit contestable, insight: "A person is jealous of everyone, except his son and his disciple."

Jewish sources are brimming with accounts of this unique teacher-parent module. The toughest rabbis could display a touching fatherliness when their students did them proud; and the softest parents could be very decisive when bringing their offspring—often, you recall, at the ripe age of three—to the schoolroom, to long pallid days of somber study.

An informed progeny is the key to collective survival. Children—boys and girls, in distinct and unequal ways—were socialized to safeguard and convey society's cumulative wisdom. Practical know-how, customs, and narratives were thus transferred. There is a universal cultural tendency, well beyond the Jewish lore, to see all good sons and daughters as torchbearers of some kind. By contrast, the prodigal sons and the daughters "traversing their ways," the youthful rebels and angry young men, are those who threaten to puff out the flame of collective memory. To turn their backs on their fathers' and mothers' teachings. To stop telling the stories.

But consider the Jewish peculiarity: here, quite early in the day, storytelling became a text-anchored precept. Teachers taught from books. Oral wisdom transformed into written codex. From ancient times, fathers had access to some script from which to read to their sons. The "generation to generation" formula was literally carved in stone, writ on papyrus, on calfskin, and later on paper. The biblical injunction "Tell your son"—the verb is *haged*, denoting spoken utterance—

was put to writing, and the writing became canonical. A textual chain ensued, even in regard to this very precept: from Exodus 13:8 to the Jerusalem and Babylonian Talmuds, thence to Maimonides, but even more effectively—to the ever-popular Haggadah.

That little tome of Passover liturgy probably evolved since the Second Temple era, with its earliest written version hailing from Egyptian-born philosopher Saadia Gaon in the tenth century CE. A veritable dinner-table book, it conjoins an array of ancient written sources, and also the lyrics of songs caught fresh from medieval oral tradition. Haggadah means "telling," in direct reference to "Tell your son." The spoken word had been pinned down and penned into book, only to bounce back into oral utterance at the Passover table and in every synagogue. Fathers and teachers read. Sons and students listened, sang, spoke, and memorized. Mothers and daughters sat at the family table where literacy was dished out and served. Somehow, we do not believe that they were passed over.

Very early in exilic history, Jewish families understood that they must act as relays of national memory embedded in written texts. It is a common error to date the beginning of Diaspora to the last catastrophic revolt of 135 CE, but it began long before that, with Jewish communities dispersed across the Persian and Roman empires. "So those days," concludes the Book of Esther, "were to be remembered and celebrated in every generation, every family, every province and every city; and these days of Purim were not to fail from among the Jews, or their memory fade from their descendants." This text, probably hailing from the fourth century BCE, still made it to the Bible, but the Jews are already exilic and bookish, and Jewish children are already told by their parents to remember and to pass on the story. For the next two and a half millennia we will celebrate it, in merriment, with a growing assortment of particular pastries to sweeten the feast, and oral, collective reading of the scroll named after Esther, one of only two women with biblical books to their names, and in our minds not the most deserving. Nor is the story morally attractive, although it is humanly captivating, a tale of power and lies, fear and lust, blood and jeering. Also national spirit, sacrifice, and teeth-clenched collective rescue. The Feast of Purim was born, taking its place in the Jewish calendar next to the age-old Passover. Other commemorative festivals will soon follow, each with its written account of a disaster deflected, each with its special scrumptious delicacies—book and food on the table together. For two and a half millennia, Jewish children have been gorging on the festive dishes while heeding, reading, and reciting these texts of doom and salvation. The Jewish holiday in a nutshell, as the saying goes: they tried to kill us, we survived, let's eat.

What magic kept this familial temple of textual memory alive through twenty-five centuries? We think that the answer has something to do with the blend of bread and books. With that uniquely verbal breast milk. With the capacity to conjoin Moses' Tablets with Mother's Table. We think that the family holiday meal preceded the synagogue pulpit and the scholar's desk by a long stretch.

But now let us set the food aside, for a while.

Simply put, our thesis is this: in order to remain a Jewish family, a Jewish family perforce relied on words. Not any words, but words that came from books.

Jewish parents did not merely *recite* the stories, the laws, and the fundaments of faith in the family circle; they *read* them. For even if they did not own any books, the ritual texts they recounted were written in books. A papyrus or a parchment was an expensive household appliance in late antiquity and in the Middle Ages, and we cannot possibly assume that every Jewish home, in northern Africa or in Europe, could own even one such item. But the synagogue held the Torah scroll tucked in the gilded closet at the wall facing Jerusalem. And someone in the vicinity—the rabbi, the schoolteacher, the physician, the rich merchant—must have owned at least some of the sacred and rabbinical books. So the tomes were within reach, oral reading and recitation was the norm, and thus their contents could resonate in every Jewish home.

Even if no synagogue was to be found within many miles, and no rabbis, someone at home would have been able to recite crumbs of Torah, crucial verses, basic formulations, and the skeleton of the Story. Maybe only a chant. They could still pass on to their progeny a written legacy, albeit in oral form. Even when bookless or barely literate, Jews were always texted.

On the other hand, if a Jewish home was reasonably well-to-do, as was that of Glikl of Hameln's merchant family in seventeenth-century Hamburg-Altona, daughters were educated too, and even went to heder for girls. "My father educated his children, sons and daughters both, in things heavenly and wordly," Glikl wrote. She grew up to be a successful businesswoman and an avid reader, mostly of Yiddish (which Glikl and her contemporaries called *Taytsh*), although she knew Hebrew and possibly also German. Her bookshelf, as evidenced in her letters, was perforce not hugely diverse, but still intellectually gluttonous: translation of the Bible, moral tracts, practical manuals, historical records of Jewish life and persecutions against Jews, Yiddish proverbs, fables, and tales —quite a broad selection of titles intended for lay readers— and then, especially for literate women, books of prayers and supplications (*tekhines*), and the hugely successful *Tzena urena*. The latter, compiled by Jacob ben Isaac Ashkenazi, gave learned women like Glikl a peek into Talmudic and Rabbinical interpretations, placed alongside the original scriptural texts for their perusal. Glikl of Hameln's life was exceptional— she was wealthy, well connected, and a gifted author of family letters which survived—but her reading materials were available to a great many Jewish women, and men too, outside the rabbinical track. Unlike its equivalents in contemporary European vernaculars, this Yiddish bookshelf was intimately linked to its scholarly neighbor, and thus fit to educate laypersons of intellectual bent.

While other premodern societies preserved their memory in a pattern we can dub "parent-story-child," the Jewish equivalent was "parent-*book*-story-child." The Jewish stories were not only narrative and moral but also legal: they presented divine laws and intricate rules of behavior. Books thus affected in-home acculturation. Books resounded in children's ears in their stiff and demanding, yet rich and sustaining, wordiness. Many of the words, of course, were cyclical, forever reread and re-uttered. The Jewish calendar lays down its daily, weekly, monthly, and annually recurring texts. Repetition can drain creativity, for sure, but it also has the strange ability to anchor, nurture, and even surprise. Reiterated lines sometimes beget music; and much of Jewish musicality grew from the resonance of repeated words. Children are prone to absorb such early textual sonorities like precious lullabies, for life.

Jewish parenting had, perhaps still has, a unique academic edge. Being a parent meant performing some level of text-based teaching, and being a child involved a certain minimum of study, at least reciting a few formulae. This meant cultural survival. Twentieth-century stereotypes, especially in the United States and to some extent in Israel, cast Jewish parents, chiefly mothers, as overbearing and emotional purveyors of anxiety and guilt. The present authors are not fussy about Jewish mother jokes—they can be very loving as well as rather funny—but our historical perspective is different. There is indeed a great fearfulness in Jewish parental genes—for many good reasons—and also an imposing set of demands. It is heavyweight, content-laden parenting.

The children were made to inherit not only a faith, not only a collective fate, not only the irreversible mark of circumcision, but also the formative stamp of a library. It was not enough for the youngsters to follow the universal rites of passage—watch and emulate their elders, learn how to work or fight, and heed ancestral tales and songs by the fireside. Oral traditions and physical emulation could not suffice. You had to read from the books, too.

Thus, for many centuries, Jewish children, girls as well as boys, were exposed to written texts: a bit of Bible, the odd Hebrew word, a few blessings and prayers. At any given moment two or three generations cohabited in the home, the synagogue, and the schoolroom. They were able to pass on the words, the songs, and the rituals. Alongside the general child-rearing practices—habit forming, skill training, and storytelling—the old generations made sure that their children and grandchildren took over the texts. "That I may cause those that love me to inherit substance, and that I may fill their treasuries," as Proverbs put it, and Rabban Yohanan aptly applied to the legacy of books.

Jesus of Nazareth, a Jew, told his disciples: "Suffer little children to come unto me, and forbid them not, for of such is the kingdom of God." The directive sounds very Jewish, but the reasoning is quintessentially Christian: it rests on the assumption that the least learned are the purest of human beings. It bonds innocence with ignorance.

But Jewish tradition usually—some Hasidic tales offer an exception—found nothing angelic in an untaught child. Jewish angels (*mal'achim*) are servers of the Lord, abstract beings representing knowledge, truth, justice, and peace, perhaps winged but impalpable, far removed from the chunky baby cherubs of Christian art. And kids are no angels. So in Jewish communities young children were already scholars. The Talmud endearingly calls them "school-babes," *tinokot shel beit rabban*. Their charm lay in their learning, their sweet fumbling with the aleph-beit, not in their untainted innocence.

Solomon, or whoever wrote Proverbs—an author evidently obsessed with the concept of wisdom, notably his own —said that a wise son makes his father glad, and a foolish son is his mother's grief. There may be no solution for the foolish (*ksil*), but consider the Hebrew term for "innocent," *tam* or *tamim*. The original biblical term meant "whole" or "untarnished," and could apply to a sacrificial animal as well as to a righteous man. But later, tellingly, *tam* became the Haggadah's simpleton. A child who must patiently be taught the Jewish fundaments. Ignorance and naïveté have no merit. There is no *sancta simplicitas* for the Jews.

Why is asking questions a favorite Jewish pastime?

Biblical Hebrew knew no question marks, but the Book of Books is full of questions. We haven't counted them all, but judging by the prevalence of whats and hows and whos and whys, it may well be the most inquisitive of holy scriptures. Quite a few, to be sure, are rhetorical, proclaiming God's glory. God himself is a great interrogator. The answers to some of his questions may seem self-evident, but they are not. Modern readers can still ponder them like deep unsettling riddles. Such are the first questions ever asked.

God to Adam: "Where are you?" and: "Who told you you are naked?"

God to Eve, and later to Cain: "What have you done?"

God to Cain: "Where is Abel your brother?"

And Cain, the first man ever to answer a question with a question, brazenly irreverent, darker than the darkest shade of chutzpah: "Am I my brother's keeper?"

Yes, brother, you are. Or are you?

And the child reads. This is not children's literature. Children's literature is modern. The boys in the old Jewish schoolroom read of Eve and the Snake and Adam, they read of Cain and Abel, they read the questions, and they question the questions. They have to face Cain's response from the same angle that God and the grownups must face it.

Other biblical inquiries display all-too-human sensitivities, not least God's own sensitivities. See his query to Abraham, "Wherefore did Sarah laugh?" The Supreme Being seriously takes offense at an old woman's disbelief in his promise of a baby. But I didn't laugh, the somewhat-frightened Sarah protests. You did too, God retorts.

Other questions are rhetorically furious: "Who asked this of you, to trample my court?" asks Isaiah, fuming on behalf of God. "Why did you let our people cross the Jordan, only to be lost at the hands of the Amorites?" asks Joshua, fuming against God. "Why did you cheat me? You are Saul!" the angry Witch of En Dor tells the disguised king of Israel, fuming on her own behalf.

But numerous biblical queries are genuinely interrogative. Some of these are intellectually spellbinding. "That which is, is far off, and exceeding deep; who can find it out?" "Will you indeed demolish the righteous along with the wicked?" "What profit has man of all his labor that he labors under the sun?" "For what advantage has the wise man over the fool?" "Why is the way of the wicked successful, and all the treacherous are safe?" And the most enchanting of the lot: "What is the way of the wind?"

There are gigantic questions and dwarfish questions. For the Talmudists, with their unquenchable legalistic curiosity, nothing was too small to be scrutinized. Why does a camel have a short tail? How did Moses know where Joseph was buried? What should be done with an egg laid during a sacred holiday? What happens when a mouse enters a house that was already cleared of leavened bread, prior to Passover, with a bit of pastry in its mouth? And if you later see a mouse leaving the house with similar loot, how can you tell it is the same mouse or the same pastry?

Some of these questions sound funny, perhaps intentionally so, serving at least two intellectual purposes. First, brain teasing: you acquire the practice of inquisitiveness by leaving no stone unturned. Second, the Talmud constantly suspends some of our normal perspectives of size and importance. In God's world, the tiniest things matter as much as the greatest. Delving into the intricate laws governing the most minuscule particles of human existence is an act of faith.

In addition, the rabbis obviously had a sense of humor. They played with ideas, made fun of colleagues and ancestors, and parodied their own learning. There is much about the Talmud that alienates the present authors, but not its humor. Nor its fondness for the seemingly trivial.

Modern Jews, tottering on the brink of faith and apostasy, asked darker questions. "Identity" is a modern concept; its crises are modern crises. As soon as you left the childhood certainties of Jewish tradition, the fatherly embrace and entrapping of rabbinical education, the motherly conjoining of nurture and ritual—while still remembering them—you found yourself on the lonely shores of tormented modernity, with all its dynamic stimulations and irretrievable losses. A generation thus huddled between the old synagogue and the new wide world, between authority and uncertainty, between Enlightenment and Holocaust. All these trajectories were intersected by faith and its demise. Haim Nahman Bialik was caught in the maze, and so were Isaac Bashevis Singer and almost every other thinker and author of that first great mass of modern Jews.

The novelist among us, in his book on Shmuel Yosef Agnon, wrote thus:

Beyond all differences in talent, perhaps we may say that the trauma, the rift, in Agnon's soul was deeper and more painful than those [other writers']; hence the creative tension, the vigor of the sources of energy, the depth of the torments are of a different order altogether. For Agnon's pain and the distress of his generation were malignant: incurable, insoluble, inextricable. There is One Who hears our prayer or there is not. There is Justice and there is a Judge or there is not. All the acts of our forefathers are meaningful or they are not. And while we're at it—is there meaning to our own acts or isn't there? And is there any meaning in any act at all? What is sin and what is guilt and what is righteousness? In all these, Agnon is neither guide nor model, but he and his heroes run around from one extreme to another in dread and despair. Such dread and such despair are the source of great works of literature in other nations as well, in other languages and in other times. And with all the restraint that imbues Agnon's writing, writing that comes "after the writer has immersed himself in ice water" ("The Tale of the Scribe"), with all the moderation and dissimulation and muting and circumlocution and irony and sometimes even sophistry—with all that, the sensitive reader will hear a muffled scream . . . an open wound. For there is a genuine creator here.

Agnon acutely felt the brink. "I stood at times among the worshippers, at times among those who question," he wrote in his story "Tehila." He should have known, of course, that some worshippers are questioners too. But Agnon had a different set of questions in mind, those of the fresh doubter, losing his religion. Perhaps he sensed that mainstream Orthodox Judaism had forgotten the spirit of questioning that the Talmud once knew.

Of all questions, the most hoped-for is the intergenerational quizzing that ensures the passing of the torch. "If your son asks you tomorrow, What are the testimonies, and the statutes, and the ordinances, which the Lord our God had commanded you?" This is the key, the Jewish Philosopher's Stone. It is the pedagogical module of memory, harking back to the national cradle, the Book of Exodus. Please, Son, ask me.

Note that the son's question is not a mere setup. To be sure, the child already accepts "our God," but he, or indeed she, is not yet bound to the plethora of obligations that "God had commanded you," the parent. Jewish adolescents have always been allowed a flicker of probing irreverence. Even in the most reverent of texts. We like them this way, both the kids and the text.

Debate and dispute are ingrained onto the process of reading. Jewish scholarship was, and is, enthusiastically disputative. We shall return to this. Let us dwell a little further on the topic of questions.

Some modes of questioning are straightforward learning tools, with a pedagogical agenda not dissimilar to the Catholic catechism. Another famous mode of Jewish questioning is geared to serve the community, as in most of the rabbinical responsa genre, the traditional question-and-answer records that form a workaday documentation of observant life. Rabbi, is this chicken kosher for our Sabbath meal?

Higher up the scholarly scale, questions and problems—*kushiot,* "tough ones" in Talmudic language—were intellectually daring. The toughest among them could easily be seen as toying with blasphemy. In privileged spaces—synagogue, yeshiva, rabbinical home—texts were studied through disputation and competing interpretations. Talmudic sons, biological or metaphorical, constantly challenge their fathers. It was a highly exclusive intellectual lineage, of course. Not everyone was invited to dispute tough problems, let alone raise them. Talmudic scholars were tagged by their mental eligibility to enter those vast scholarly thickets. The spiritual *pardes,* the orchard of learning, was both a metaphor and an acronym for a steep scale of intellectual challenge and psychological danger. Venturing deeper into the orchard meant you could pose and ponder tougher questions, peruse secret wisdom, but also risk losing your life or your mind in the process.

Let us return to the children, nibbling food and words at the family table or clustered around their *melamed* in the schoolroom. The Talmud stipulated, and the Haggadah later popularized, some family rules of discussion. It was a paradigm of intergenerational quizzing: youngsters ask questions, and their elders reply. At the Passover table, when reading from the Haggadah itself, queries and answers are preformulated and preassigned. The smallest child sings the "Four Questions," and the whole family retorts with the answers. But note that despite its formulaic nature, the Haggadah recognizes, and banks on, a habitual dynamic of tough intellectual interrogation. The child's simple queries are dubbed *kushiot,* tough ones, just like the truly challenging Talmudic conundrums.

In another favorite Passover take on inquisitive youngsters, "The Four Sons," the Haggadah relates that three out of the four sons—the wise, the wicked, and the simple—pose rather difficult questions of their own accord. Since the sons represent distinct intellectual types, the questions vary in sophistication and learning, but each merits an individualized response. Only the last son, "he who does not know how to ask," has to be approached by the parent ("you broach it to him"). Most interesting by far is the "wicked" son: "What is this work to you?" he snaps. In modern eyes this is a perfectly typical noncommittal teenager. Other traditional cultures would have had the lad flogged. Not that Jewish fathers never administered corporal punishment, but around the Passover table the "wicked son" gets a verbal response, albeit a rather tough one, signaling that the parent is refusing to give up on that straying scion. Passing on the torch involves a smart approach to adolescent adversity.

We are not trying to glorify all ancient Jewish teaching habits. They were neither liberal nor modern, neither egalitarian nor pluralistic. This sort of parent-child exchange hinges on set truths. It penalizes what it regards as wickedness or stupidity, and what we might regard as open-mindedness and originality. But look at the better side of this question-based education: it was spirited, it was playful, it was about ideas, it encouraged curiosity, and it required reading. It compelled very young children to read, and at the same time it showed them how compelling reading can be. It stipulated that even the simpleton, and even the wicked, deserved answers, not just penalties. Not bad, we think, for a premodern family table.

What about daughters?

Daughters vary. The biblical are not akin to the Talmudic. The former can be active and influential, the latter far less so. But consider the table, that homespun family device relaying texts through generations. Daughters, female relatives, perhaps also servants, were present at the table when texts from the holy books were being read or recited. And since the torch was made of words, girls were eminently capable of picking it up and passing it on. We will discuss Jewish women at some length. For now suffice it to say that the present authors are not the first father-and-daughter team to try their hand at a Jewish intergenerational conversation.

On many of the themes of this book, we are arguing for a continuum. A long line of descent.

This, in our case, is not a religious thought. We see no mysterious necessity, historical or divinely ordained, for the Jews to have come such a long way. Contingency may have played a role. Perhaps we owe our survival to a handful of early Christian scholars who decided to include the Hebrew Bible in the Christian canon. Perhaps also to a few early Muslim jurists who decided to extend the Jews a measure of toleration. In several junctures in history, our existence as a dynasty of believers and story-carriers might have been extinguished. This is by no means unthinkable.

But once the Jewish creed and narrative were allowed to live on, despite numerous and cruel disruptions to life and worship, the hidden engine proved so strong and alluring that it kept many Jews staunchly Jews. It proved so persuasive that it held bright youngsters in the ghetto or the shtetl, the mellah (Jewish quarter in Moroccan towns) or the Street of the Jews, poor and dismal as they were. Centuries passed, they migrated, they moved, they ran, they trudged, and they carried the books on their backs.

The most prominent religious phrasing of this theme is that the Torah guards the Jews insofar as they keep and heed the Torah. An alternative version is that the Sabbath saves them, as long as they observe the Sabbath.

Our own take is not radically different, even though we have no divine sanction upholding either Sabbath or Torah. What kept the Jews going were the books.

Of course the books were considered holy; but turn this around, and you will see a people who loved the books so much that they consecrated them. So what came first, sanctity or scroll? We hold one answer and the faithful hold another. But it is also worth noting that after the destruction of the Second Temple, only books remained sacrosanct, and certain words. Nothing else. No temple, no relic, no apostolic dynasty. Rabbis are only human. Holy statues and pictures are out of the question. Driven far from Jerusalem, bereft of Tabernacles and Menorah, only the books remained.

So when you ran for your life from massacre and pogrom, from burning home and synagogue, it was children and books you took with you. The books and the children.

Alongside the sacred texts flourished the profane: the uncanonical, the Midrashic, the poetic, and in modern times the downright unholy. There were books for scholars and books for plain folk, for the barely literate and for the philosophically minded. In the early modern era books for women appeared, but long before that time Jewish women were already treated to a few texts created specifically for their erudition and pleasure. Similarly, children's books are a modern invention, but long before modernity, playful texts were deftly inserted into the Haggadah to amuse the tiniest Jews and draw them into their parents' library. From the late Middle Ages, illuminated books must have appealed to readers big and small, but until late modern times—until Chagall, more or less—Jewish images could never stand alone. Jews were not allowed the iconic self-sufficiency of pagan and Christian images. Even where the biblical prohibition of statues and pictures could be side-stepped, it permitted the images only to serve the words, illustrate their meanings, and mirror their story.

But books would remain frail corporeal objects, and holy books mere flammable fetishes, without the act of reading. In a beautiful and terrible poem, Bialik salutes the decaying old scrolls in the abandoned synagogue of his childhood shtetl, or in the deserted yeshiva of his youth: "ancients of dust," "eternally dead." Incessant reading, whether purely repetitive or freshly interpretive, was the only act that retained, rebooted, and reconsecrated the texts. There was collective reading and individual reading, wielding the scroll-pointer and orally reciting, knowing-by-heart and reading-in-the-heart, *nigun*-humming and melody-chanting and voice-raising and soundless lip-moving. There was reading as prayer, reading as ritual, reading as messaging, and reading as reasoning.

No other premodern people were systematically exposed, in this way, to written texts in their homes across a broad social spectrum. In-house reading was a rare and unusual practice in Europe of the Middle Ages, due to poverty and illiteracy. It may have been more common in the Muslim world, but not as a family practice. In Jewish households, fathers and mothers, grandfathers and grandmothers, prayed and blessed and narrated, recited and sang. They went through a fairly large corpus of texts over and over again. The children ate and drank and watched and listened. At the age of twelve for girls and thirteen for boys, they received full responsibility for the textual legacy, for obeying the precepts and for keeping the *Brit*.

This piece of social history is, to us, the single most important fact about the survival of the Jews. At the youngest age, when words can be magical and stories spellbinding, a unique vocabulary came along with the sweet and savory Sabbath-meal offerings. How can anyone measure the cultural impact of the premeal grace, *yehi shem adonai mevorach me'ata ve'ad olam,* in Hebrew from time immemorial, in father's Sephardi or Ashkenazi intonation, along with the sweet challah bread from mother's oven? And the songs? And the stories, outlandish, awful, and delightful?

Of course, not only in the Jewish hippocampus do texts and tastes inhabit neighboring neurons. Other cultures mixed verse and lore, food and festivities. Perhaps all human traditions were formed in much the same way. But as we imagine those bookish tables and those verbal meals, we seem to understand how they must have imprinted a particularly strong connectivity on infant minds.

We nonbelievers remain Jews by reading, too. This is not a matter of pure choice, of course. Many other factors have made us what we are: parents, Zionism, modernity, Hitler, habit, and luck. But if there is any chain at all between Abraham and us, it is made of written words. Like our ancestors, we are texted. And—if one further liberty with the English language is permitted—we are texted to our ancestors. We are the Atheists of the Book.

Israeli Jews have benefited from a window of opportunity unprecedented in Jewish or Western history. A century ago, the men and women who laid the foundations of modern Israel and modernized the Hebrew language also put together a school syllabus that included broad nonreligious Bible study. These pioneers were mostly secular, but only recently secular. Their biblical curriculum harked to German philology and modern literary criticism. But its greatest asset was the new accessibility of Hebrew. One can argue about the connections between Ancient and Modern Hebrew, and doubt our capability to truly understand biblical vocabulary; but the sheer beauty and power of biblical literature truly dazed some of those new Hebrew-speaking children. Including us.

This lasted three generations. We doubt whether most Israeli kids today are still hooked by Genesis, and whether teenagers are still astounded by Job. For several decades now, Modern Hebrew, both language and literature, is stepping away from biblical inspirations. For some liberals, the Bible has become a nationalist domain. Nevertheless, most of Israel's Hebrew speakers still have some *Tanach* in them. There are, to date, more Bible-wise atheists in Israel than anywhere else.

This gives us some edge. Most Western nonbelievers today have not crossed paths with the Bible as a literary text. Unlike Homer, it is not widely taught in schools. Like Twitter, it is handed down in byte-size chunks. Most biblical quotations in circulation are not longer than a verse. Increasingly, such Bible snippets are associated with priests, pastors, pulpits, and American presidents.

The paradox is clear to an Israeli eye: today, in many secular societies, religion itself obscures this exquisite work of art from view. The Constitution of the United States helps bar it from public schools, because it is mistaken for a (wholly, solely) religious text. This is a sad cultural loss.

As Jewish atheists, we take religion to be a great human invention. As such it is neither falsehood nor forgery. A skeptic might grasp the Jewish scriptures, like other holy texts, as an apocryphal web of prejudices. A Marxist might deem them tools of oppression, although in this case the oppressors were, *nebbish,* no grander than a convoy of frail and tattered rabbis. A multiculturalist will find nothing in the Bible that is less or more interesting than any other ethnocultural endeavor.

But by our secular lights these scriptures and their textual progeny are a legacy of collective human greatness. That is because we are privileged with a new vista of amazement. Precisely the critical, selective, and discerning reading, the modern and secular reading, can generate a sense of awe. Speakers of Modern Hebrew, a language barely one century old, have been granted a brand new ticket to an ancient cultural spectacle. And the nonbelievers among them may gasp at the notion that this spectacle has no divine scriptwriter-producer. Backstage, thousands upon thousands of historical players and authors are at work, all strictly human, inhabiting a trimillennial line. This is breathtaking.

We don't like all of it. We don't ascribe either historical factuality or scientific certainty to much of it. We are not morally bound by any of it. But we find so much that is true, good, and insightful in parts of the Jewish bookshelf, that we can claim to have replaced faith with wonder.

Let us discuss unease.

Jewish sensitivities, obsessions, and hang-ups are by no means restricted to Jews, nor are they common to all Jews. As Sigmund Freud commented when asked about his coreligionists' neurotic tendency, "Gentiles have plenty of neuroses too. Only the Jew is more sensitive, more critical of himself, more dependent on the judgment of others. He has less self-confidence than the Gentiles, and is fresher—has more 'chootzpa' too—both come from the same thing." Thus, for Freud, there may not have been a unique set of Jewish neuroses, but there certainly was a unique Jewish proneness to them.

Every Jewish trait can be explained in psychohistorical terms. In the modern era it dawned on some minds that Jewishness is an apt parable for mankind at large. The "Wandering Jew" is no longer an accursed exception but a fundamental global type. "All men are Jews," Bernard Malamud reportedly quipped, "though few men know it." The very universality of certain Jewish worries, especially in modern times, accounts for the underlying humanity of those Jewish worries. If the modern world has adopted such Jewish characteristics as existential angst, nomadic restlessness, multilinguality, and mediating capacities—then the modern world can also cry with Primo Levi, laugh with Mel Brooks, and do both with Philip Roth.

Some aspects of Jewish sensitivity, however, belong not to the realm of psychology but to the trickier paths of creativity, intellectual legacy, and cultural staying power.

Certain patterns of conduct crop up wherever Jewish creativity holds sway, especially but not solely in modern times. The first is a peculiar talkativeness. Think of the interplay of oral and written traditions in biblical and Talmudic times. The sealing of books never trumped the love of speaking. Jews have been prone to wordiness in times of mortal danger or abundant ease, when facing God, their spouses, or the local lord of the manor, when hailing fellow Jews or complete strangers. It is a nervous and alert verbosity that coils itself around ancient texts with novel formulations. Jews talk a lot, quote a lot, and dispute a lot: this has always been the case.

Almost everything else stems from this wordiness. True, biblical characters are far less verbose than ancient Greek protagonists, but utterances have stronger impact, sometimes even history-changing force, in the biblical narrative. It begins with God creating the world by a series of succinct utterances, and Adam claiming rule over the animals by naming them. (Adam also names his wife, after she kick-starts human history by luring him to the tree of knowledge; but the Bible does not link that act of naming to dominion.)

Think of the Abraham-to-Seinfeld, or the Sarah–to–Hannah Arendt, proneness to argument. Jewish literature, from scripture to stand-up, displays a recurring love of the counterproposition, the answerback, the chutzpah. And this talkative irreverence is rooted in a constant habit of rational (if emotive) deliberation, and a deep sense of the importance of words. Jews have always tried to reason with others, even if those others played by different rules, nonverbal, irrational, bluntly physical and violent. When an opponent was particularly formidable or menacing, the Jewish attempt at verbal persuasion may have been tremulous, but it remained staunch.

That may be why Shakespeare, perhaps in spite of himself, gave the best piece of oratory in *The Merchant of Venice* to the otherwise-despicable Shylock himself:

> I am a Jew. Hath not a Jew eyes? Hath not a Jew hands, organs, dimensions, senses, affections, passions; fed with the same food, hurt with the same weapons, subject to the same diseases, heal'd by the same means, warm'd and cool'd by the same winter and summer, as a Christian is? If you prick us, do we not bleed? If you tickle us, do we not laugh? If you poison us, do we not die? And if you wrong us, do we not revenge?

Revenge may or may not ensue, but effusive, loquacious Reason is assuredly there, mouthed in a desperate attempt to bridge the Jew's insular "otherness" with the mainland of human normality. It often ended calamitously, words silenced by a blow.

For some modern observers, Jewish "abnormality" is the origin of Jewish verbosity. Philip Roth, in a book named after the selfsame Shylock, has an interlocutor explaining Jewish talkativeness as a symptom of perpetual duplicity and multiplicity, hinging between worlds and eons, so that "inside each Jew there were so many speakers! Shut up one and the other talks. Shut him up and there is a third, a fourth, a fifth Jew with something more to say."

Some of these inner Jews will always be conversing with (or shouting at) their ancestors, from parents to Patriarchs. Or struggling with texts their ancestors produced, with the ideas their ancestors promulgated. This habit can account for what this book is doing. This is why we feel entitled to place ancient

Hebrews and modern Jews on one linear continuum, not a biological one, not an ethnic one, not even a religious continuum, but a verbal one. So many parents produced so many texts for us to converse with, polemicize against, or, in Roth's terms, try in vain to "shut up."

Beyond the psychological origins and the emotional mayhem of Jewish wordiness lies a cerebral confidence that is neither tremulous nor neurotic. Freud, who explained the sensitivity and the chutzpah of Jews as a survival strategy serving an unconfident people, saw only a part of their frame of mind. For there is also an analytical mechanism at work, incorporating great trust in reason and a peculiar sense of self. The arguing subject is never a mere platform of feelings, experiences, and traumas. He or she is also the active seeker of truth, the bold asserter of reason. Not mere survival instinct but also an intellect is at work. Jews display a deeply rooted belief in the power of words to create and re-create reality, at times through prayer but at least as often by argumentative truth-seeking.

This ties into the Jewish quest for social, economic, and political equity. A quirky pursuit of justice runs from the social-minded prophet Moses to nineteenth-century socialist thinker Moses Hess. This quest has been called *tikkun olam*, roughly translatable as setting the world to rights, hailing from the Kabbalism of Rabbi Isaac Luria, the Holy Ari. In Kabbalah, the *tikkun* involves the spiritual mending of our piecemeal world after the "Breaking of the Vessels," a divine and moral catastrophe. In the twentieth century, Israeli children would cry "the vessels are broken!" whenever the rules of the game were infringed.

Restless justice-seeking has been called many other names, too. In modern times it has flowed into mainstream socialism, liberalism, and communitarianism. It can pertain to the traditional self-sustaining Jewish society, the *kahal* or *kehila,* but it also provided a starting point for the major Western lineages of universalism and humanism. There is something deeply emotional about this mission—take a look at Isaiah 5 for a moving account of injustice—but it is a rational pursuit nonetheless. Evil, for some prophets and Talmudic sages, was like an illogical statement, or like bad geometry. Honesty was a straight line, and crookedness was crooked.

Another closely related offshoot of the Jewish way with words is humor. Modern Jews probably display more humor than their ancient forebears, at least if we go by written evidence. Still, the second Patriarch was named Isaac, "He who will laugh," because both his parents laughed at the divine promise for a child in Sarah's barren old age. As we have mentioned, Sarah and God embark on a rather amusing argument on that occasion: "Then Sarah denied, saying: 'I laughed not'; for she was afraid. And He said: 'Nay; but thou didst laugh.'" How many religions began with God playing a game of "you did, too" with the ancestral matriarch?

Ecclesiastes, said to be King Solomon, took a dim view of merriment: "I said of laughter: 'It is mad'; and of mirth: 'What doth it accomplish?'" The Bible's terse, stark, magnificently concise Hebrew is seldom jocular. In fact, some of the funnier people in the Bible are not Hebrews at all. The Philistine Achish, King of Gath, lands a good punch when he dismisses David, who plays the fool in his court: "Wherefore do ye bring him to me?" Achish scolds his servants. "Do I lack madmen, that ye have brought this fellow to play the madman in my presence?" This turn of phrase bears an uncanny resemblance to Yiddish (*nu, oych mir a meshugener*). Did ancient Philistine wit somehow feed into medieval German-Jewish dialect? This is a nice thought. We often notice that present-day Israelis and Palestinians share a common sense of humor.

Frequently biting, indeed self-biting, and sometimes outright self-derisive, Yiddish made Jewish humor into an art, and Groucho Marx and Woody Allen transformed it into a universal brand. Freud did not explain why among Jews fear, anger, or despondency is so often and so effectively detonated into wit. Jewish humor is almost always verbal, and thus it is characteristically far more Groucho than Harpo. Body language, though richly employed, has almost always served as a vehicle for funny words. Pantomime is almost un-Jewish.

Argumentativeness and humor breed that other Jewish trait, irreverence. Rather peculiarly for a people of staunch faith, and certainly untypical of other monotheistic religions, Jewish chutzpah targets prophet and rabbi, judge and king, gentile and coreligionist. Its earliest recorded target was the Almighty himself. This irreverence can dovetail with devotion in a way distinctly alien to other systems of faith, and displays a temperament more democratic, not to say anarchic, than other systems of politics.

There is something adolescent, eternally puerile, about some Jewish attitudes to God, rabbis, and worldly authority. The book of Genesis is full of fathers and mothers of various sorts, as well as a plethora of offspring, all under the fatherly gaze of the Creator. There is plenty of sibling rivalry and intergenerational bickering. Tellingly, the term *family* in the

Bible is often equivalent to *nation*. And of all the "families of the earth," as the prophet Amos put it, the Israelite family considered itself closest to God and most accountable to him: "You only have I known of all the families of the earth; therefore I will visit upon you all your iniquities." Note how family, nationhood, verbal imperative, and accountability—hence, guilt—are knotted together from a very early time.

This feeds back into the great sensitivity we have already touched upon: the children.

For countless generations Jewish men and women experienced great fear, often well founded, for the lives of their offspring. But not exclusively for their lives. The fear was always coupled with a staunch refusal to let one's children off the hook—and off the book—of Jewish destiny. "Tell your son" has a dark side: your son and daughter become the carriers of an ancient curse, the bearer of a sad story, and, of course, liable to everything that threatened a medieval or a modern Jew. All the chicken soup in the world cannot immunize them from this liability.

Another theme escorting every significant phase of Jewish history is the sheer multitude of strong personalities. Active, stubborn, vocal men and women people the biblical records, the Mishnaic and Talmudic eras, the Babylonian centuries, the golden age of Sepharad, the earliest origins of Ashkenaz, and every modern chapter in Jewish history. All histories are made by strong persons, of course, but those were not textbook heroes. Often exuding tremendous human weakness, more often than not on the wrong side of history, shouldering their common legacy of text and recollection, bound on the insertion of meaning into their own lives and the lives of others. And there are so many of them, so many whom we know by name and often by personality.

To be sure, the Greeks had more gods, but the Hebrew Bible registered more humans. There are far more active protagonists in the Old Testament than in the New, more Mishnaic Tannaim and Talmudic Amoraim than all recorded Greek and Roman thinkers put together. We are talking about sheer numbers, not about quality of output. The Talmudists were not necessarily better thinkers, nor the biblical heroes braver or wiser, than their classical counterparts.

But note how many people, real and historical people, are crowding the ancient Hebrew pages. No author would want to invent so many protagonists, many of whom are named without having any significant role in the plot. Talmudic sages are on record in their hundreds—some scholars put it at thousands—each with his particular wisdom. Medieval rabbis were named, quoted, and revered at a time when Christendom granted little or no credit to individual authorship. Numerous and differing characters keep speaking up and elbowing their way into Jewish history. And Jewish history, from the king's scribe to the modern authors, was particularly good at recording names, delineating personalities, and sounding individual voices.

The historical threads gathered here are neither exhaustive nor conclusive. Not that all the features we peruse appeared in every Jewish time or place. But certain themes keep cropping up in the annals of the Jews. They are our longitudes.

If the Word—spoken and written, recited and quoted—is

the true key of Jewish continuity, then any attempt to build or demolish a physical Jewish pedigree must be set aside. Regardless of the imperative of marrying within the fold, asserted from Ezra and Nehemiah to current orthodoxy, Jewish continuity has never been about bloodlines. The authors of this book, perhaps partially descended from those emblematic Khazars and Cossacks, have nothing to say about a presumed genetic, racial, or ethnic continuity of the Jews. We are not into noses. We are not into chromosomes, fascinating as their study may be. Our story "does not need this hypothesis," as Pierre-Simon Laplace once told Napoleon. Nor do we need the hypothesis of God's existence (actually, this is what Laplace was talking about), or of the divine guidance of Jewish fate. Our story is not about the role of God but about the role of words. God is one of those words.

Thus the recurring themes that render Jewish continuity so persuasive are lined up along a written and verbal genealogy. One cannot be a Jew without exposure to a certain lexicon. The relevant terminology was put in writing almost from the very start—first on stone, then in scrolls, later in codices, now on screen. Jewish writing, sacred and profane, benefited enormously (though seldom solely) from previous Jewish writing. The People of the Book therefore display long lineages that make perfect sense. If you are a reader.

Our view of our history in terms of verbal genealogies may explain why we chose to write this essay as a father-and-daughter team and, no less important, a writer-and-historian team. "The past is a foreign country," wrote L. P. Hartley, and David Lowenthal made this quotation into a sound historiographical statement. Indeed, much of the Jewish past, amid much of all human past, is also strange and discomfiting for us.

Let's pick four figures, almost at random: the prophetess Deborah, King Rehoboam, Rabbi Akiva, and Rabbi Abraham Isaac Kook. This ensemble is considerably spread out on the Jewish timeline: the twelfth century BCE (perhaps), the tenth century BCE (perhaps), the first and second centuries CE, and the nineteenth and twentieth centuries CE. None of these grand persons is close to the present authors in terms of their material and moral world. Their life contexts are, to differing degrees, alien to us. Their behavior, views, or decisions might seem bizarre, astonishing, or even obnoxious to us. One suspects that each of the four would feel equally alien to the others, had they met in some ahistorical space. Their dress, language, and attitudes would differ dramatically. They would not even speak the same language.

Except, of course, that they would understand some Hebrew. They would understand each other's names, all hailing from biblical originals or roots. Deborah being the earliest, the three men might be willing—and able!—to converse with her in her own early Hebrew. Moreover, they will have common topics of conversation: Jacob and the twelve tribes, Moses and Mount Sinai, the Land of Israel and its natural and human geography. Quite likely, their respective pronunciations of names would be markedly different, but not unabridgeably so. Furthermore, each of them would certainly know of each of the others who preceded him. Deborah may stare at Rabbi Kook's attire in disbelief, but the two rabbis and the king would look at Deborah in admiring recognition, never mind her un-shtetl-like dress.

All four will share an identity centered on Israelite descent, a strong will, a powerful commitment to their ancestry, a great concern for their posterity, and a wonderful way with words. Even Rehoboam, with his loutish quips—"My little finger is thicker than my father's loins"; "Whereas my father chastised you with whips, so shall I chastise you with scorpions"—is something of a despot-poet. Deborah would have understood every word of Rehoboam's, and so of course did Akiva and Kook. What would their politics look like? How would they engage with one another, or with the present authors, on the burning issues of Israel's requisite borders and type of government? The present authors, indeed, have political axes to grind against Akiva's disciples as well as Kook's disciples. But we would be able to converse. Some terms would be available to us all: people, law, council, covenant, boundary. Others—such as a Jewish and Democratic State—would be unknown to ancient ears, but not, we think, incomprehensible. We would be particularly curious to know what modern Israeli parties Deborah and Akiva would vote for.

Above all, each member of our quartet would fully understand, and not be in the least surprised to learn, that we are placing us all on one continuum.

Distance and difference should not be underplayed. As far as we are concerned, there is nothing mystical or miraculous—nothing divine—about the Jewish continuities. We do not admire, let alone worship, our great forebears. A few ancient Athenians are dearer to our hearts than most biblical Israelites.

Why, then, is there so much in the Jewish texts, from the most ancient ones, that rings loud, clear, and familiar to us? We are drawn to that multitude of dramatis personae inhabiting the Hebrew and Jewish texts. There is so much flesh, blood, and voice. There are occasional moments of eerie intimacy.

Such intimacy is not limited, of course, to Jewish texts. Antigone can arouse a sense of personal recognition, Saint Augustine can generate an emotional response, Don Quixote can articulate deep sentiments, and almost nothing human is alien to Chekhov. These sources are no less enthralling, no less endearing, than anything in the Jewish books. For us, parts of the Jewish past are very alien, while some non-Jewish legacies are distinctly close.

We must therefore add one more defining edge to the lineage of Jewish texts and persons. There is something singular in the past-gazing creativeness of those multitudes of literate Jews, their cumulative records, and their capacity to keep talking and making sense to each other across vast stretches of time, across languages and across cultures. They are all talking to one another. Like a constant argument at a never-ending Sabbath meal, it is not likeability or like-mindedness that keeps the flame alive; it is the lexicon of great issues and deep familiarities.

It goes without saying that we cannot tell—especially for ancient times—who was a "historical figure," and who a myth. We cannot tell who "really" did or authored whatever is claimed that they did or authored. We are curious about it, but it does not really matter. Historical truth is not archaeological truth, said Ahad Ha'am. History can convey genuine truth through fictional figures, allegories, and myths. And a fourth-century Talmudist said that the biblical Job never existed, but was a fable. Other sages argued against him, but the fictional-Job-theory was duly included in the Talmud. Why was it not wiped off the slate, as blasphemous or worthless? Because—or so we'd like to think—the Talmud anticipated and accepted our point: fables can tell a truth. Fiction is not a fib. Job existed, whether or not he "truly" existed. He exists in the minds of countless readers, who discussed him and argued about him for millennia. Job, like Macbeth and Ivan Karamazov, exists as textual truth.

What moves us is the gradual discovery that—by our lights, by our reading lights—we are heirs to such a procession of subscribers to the same ever-growing library. That the Jews, having amassed such a trove of referential buildup, having talked and written and read their way through so many ages and so many disasters, have created a genealogy of familiarity that is unique.

So for us, for example, not Rehoboam but Job is an intimate correspondent. Not Rabbi Kook the Elder but Amos the prophet and Ahad Ha'am the essayist are allies in the quest for human justice and peace. Not Deborah the gleeful amazon but Deborah the sarcastic mother is strangely recognizable to us, with her domestic fierceness, bitingly articulate. Not Rabbi Akiva who pushed his students into a doomed rebellion, but Rabbi Yehuda HaNasi, a fugitive and rescuer of scholarship, on the losing side of military history but on the winning side of intellectual history, is our political brother in arms.

These are our preferences. Every reader is bound to have others, and probably contest ours, perhaps vehemently. But if you are such a reader, Jewish or not, you are already part of our family. And all functional families, we are told, depend on putting disagreements into words.

TWO

Vocal Women

CONSIDER THE VERY beginning of the Song of Songs.

"The Song of Songs," it says, "which is Solomon's."

Is it, now? And in what way? Was it, as generations of sages and scholars have told us, written by King Solomon? Or, as modern academics claim, traditionally ascribed to King Solomon?

Perhaps it is Solomon's in a different way. Dedicated *to* Solomon. Written *for* Solomon.

By whom?

Here's an idea that makes psychological and grammatical sense to us. Let's look at the book's second verse too.

"The Song of Songs which is Solomon's. Let him kiss me with the kisses of his mouth—for thy love is better than wine."

Very beautiful, isn't it? And also rather haphazard. Note that all three grammatical persons, in singular, appear in these two compact lines. There's a "me." There's a "thy." There's Solomon and "him."

Who is speaking?

Sages and scholars tell us that the Song of Songs is an allegory, referring to God's love of Israel, and to the Jews' love of their God. This way of reading allowed a highly erotic text into the biblical canon in the first place. This is interesting, but it does not put our curiosity to rest. Who are "him," "me," and "thy"?

We are not buying the God-as-lover explanation. If Solomon is inviting God to kiss him with the kisses of his mouth, which is—to put it briefly—rather more Tel Aviv than Jerusalem, the next verses confuse us further. They point at a very physical, heterosexual attraction: "Thine ointments have a goodly fragrance . . . therefore do the maidens love thee."

So who is the speaker?

Let's show you a little magic, in Hebrew. "Which is Solomon's" is *asher li-Shlomo*. אשר לשלמה.

Now we add one character, the Hebrew alphabet's tiniest letter, *yod*. The amended verse is *ashir li-Shlomo*. אשיר לשלמה.

So the opening of our book now reads:

"The Song of Songs I shall sing to Solomon," flowing smoothly into—

"Let him kiss me with the kisses of his mouth—for thy love is better than wine."

It all falls into place if the Singer of the Song of Songs is a woman, beginning her love song to Solomon in a declaratory first person, only to move swiftly and intimately into the second person. Thy love. Thine ointments. The maidens love thee.

We are not talking historical truth here. No one knows who wrote the Song of Songs, or whether it is linked to the historical King Solomon. But we do know that language conceals secrets. By introducing one small Hebrew character to the opening line, we may have uncovered a new author. Female.

Let us call her Avishag. There was an Avishag of Shunam, a pretty young woman invited to warm the elderly David's bed at nights. The unnamed beloved of the Song of Songs is The Shunammite (or Shulamith), which may refer to the historical Avishag or to an allegorical paramour. So if our emblematic Avishag indeed penned parts of the Bible's most erotic tome, she should surely count as one of the great female poets of the Bible, alongside Miriam and Deborah, and of world literature in general, alongside Sappho and Emily Dickinson.

For a long time, the historian among us thought that the novelist among us had invented this text-turning trick, this subversive little *yod*. And maybe he did, in his turn. But happily, one or more modern scholars preceded us in positing "ashir li-Shlomo," in a female voice, as a viable alternative to the official biblical text. Nevertheless, in the history of ideas, the turning point is when a concept acquires a fresh context. Today, our vocal Shunammite is newly meaningful. We must revisit those strong female Israelites talking and singing their way up and down the Hebrew Bible, because they offer cutting-edge significance to twenty-first-century Israel and present-day Jews.

Today, some powerful Jewish communities do not wish to hear women singing. Not on stage, not in civil or military ceremonies, not even in the shower. As this book is being written, a vociferous debate is ablaze in Israel over the ultra-Orthodox Jewish demand to silence women's voices and erase or blur female images in the public sphere. Some advertisers and event producers are following suit. A woman's face, body, and especially her voice, numerous rabbis tell us, belong within the home. Virtue and modesty are at stake, especially men's. Jewish women are princesses, say the spiritual leaders, and their dignity and beauty are best kept off the streets. Doesn't the Bible tell us "All the honor of the king's daughter is indoors" (Psalms 45:14)?

It doesn't, actually. The psalm relates, in colorful detail, how Solomon's foreign brides, daughters of neighboring royalty, were *brought indoors* to the Jerusalem palace in all their festive glory. In fact, so much chic paraphernalia is listed in this particular chapter that one suspects the court scribe, presenting himself in the opening lines as the king's "ready writer," *sofer mahir*, was himself rather into this imported fashion hype. You would hardly think he wants women to remain hidden behind shutters. Stage curtains would be more his thing.

But generations of sages and rabbis have used "all the honor of the king's daughter is indoors" to keep women away from the public eye. Maimonides certainly did. A woman, he wrote in *Mishneh Torah,* is by no means a prisoner in her own home. Nevertheless,

> It is uncouth for a woman always to leave home, this time to go out and another time to go on the street. Indeed, a husband should prevent a wife from doing this and not allow her to go out more than once or twice a month, as is necessary. For there is nothing more attractive for a woman than to sit in the corner of her home, as "All the glory of the king's daughter is within." [Again Psalms 45:14, translated here in accordance with Maimonides' interpretation.]

We do not oppose the rabbinical habit, old and new, of playing around with the meanings of ancient verses. How can we? In this book we are doing much the same. But there are some differences. Unlike ultra-Orthodoxy, we are not trying to denounce, confine, or silence anyone. More to the point, our approach to the very act of interpretation is different from the traditional rabbis'. For us, the rules are something like this: Read in growing circles around your quotation rather than pluck it out of context. Cherish discovery and surprise more than your own agenda. Acknowledge the shortcomings of texts and authors you love, and the merits of those you dislike. Look hard to see the inner logic of a paragraph, a page, and a chapter.

The Bible is teeming with women "going on the streets." Sorry, Maimonides. And it has a great many women singing outdoors, to mixed audiences. Miriam sang, drummed, and possibly also danced in front of a whole people. Deborah sang her own lyrics from the very seat of government, performing a duet with her chief of staff. Hannah may have delivered her poetic thanksgiving to the almighty alone at home, but it obviously reached the media, and takes up a good part of 1 Samuel 2. These ladies, and perhaps our songstress Avishag, and the three daughters of the singing family of Heman, are just the tip of the camel. There are plenty more.

"All the women" of the Sinai generation, Exodus tells us, followed Miriam rejoicing and drumming. The first book of Samuel relates that women from "all the towns of Israel" sang, "played," and beat those drums after David slayed Goliath: "Saul hath slain his thousands, and David his ten thousands"! Ask King Saul what he thought of that nationwide female choir. We guarantee you that their gender was the least of his problems.

Yet the Hebrew grammar is notoriously chauvinistic. Male forms prevail and female forms usually trail behind, groaning under an extra suffix. If you have one man in the group and a thousand women, the plural pronoun or verb will be male. Everyone knows the Bible and its language are deeply patriarchal. We agree.

But why does the same biblical Hebrew become almost feminist when it feels like it? In several places, we are specifically told of "men-singers and women-singers." Instead of burying those female singers under the general all-male form, instead of having them all singing under the blanket masculine noun or verb, several different books, presumably written in different periods, repeatedly emphasize the female alongside the male. What accounts for this sudden sensitivity to gender?

We think we can fathom the answer. When both grammatical genders are mentioned, something is being emphasized. Take the individual case of Old Barzillai. Don't worry if you have never heard of him. He was just a well-connected octogenarian fellow who made his way into the Bible by complaining to his friend King David, as old men sometimes do, of age-related disabilities: that he could no longer tell good from evil, taste what he eats and drinks, or hear the singing of men and women. In this receding ebb of incapacity, deafness to the voice of female singers is the last blow. If you don't believe us, ask David, who evidently understood Barzillai's account of cognitive decline. So the king, as the second book of Samuel tells us, grudgingly agreed not to schlep his elderly friend with him to Jerusalem after all. The biblical author may have wished to laud David's good sense, and that was the whole point of his story; but to our ears, almost three millennia later, it is the distinct female singing that reverberates as the currently relevant punch line.

Then there is another sort of emphasis, a national one,

apparent in several biblical mentions of intersexual singing. Coming home to Zion from the Babylonian Captivity, two hundred male and female chanters marched among the repatriating Jews. Even Talmudic and post-Talmudic commentators didn't seem to mind. "Male and Female to sing on the road, for they went up in joy and promenade," explained the early modern exegete rabbi David Altschuler, or perhaps it was his son Hillel Yechiel Altschuler (their two-generation biblical commentaries are known as the *Metzudot*). Here was a shrewd insight: in male-dominated ancient Israel, celebrations were truly jubilant when men and women rejoiced together. The more mixed, the merrier.

From Miriam to Ezra, from the crossing of the Red Sea to the return from Babylon, the Bible lends its gender duality precisely to those collective moments of elation. Grammatical walls open up when the authors wish to describe how a whole people walked from slavery to liberty. For the Hebrews, freedom cut through sexual and social barriers. As did joy.

We hope we can rest our case. Let us briefly share with you two final and eclectic thoughts.

The first thought is this: patriarchal societies are not always what they seem. Paternalistic languages have tricks up their sleeves. The biblical matriarchs outnumbered their patriarch husbands four to three, and their personae are hardly less memorable. At times, if you read closely enough, you might spy an alternative grammar and story line cautiously cropping up.

And our second thought: did you notice that Rabbi David Altschuler, or perhaps his son, called the Return to Zion a "promenade" (*tiyul*)? This was quite a rare noun until Modern Hebrew took it up, although it did make one appearance in the eleventh-century Talmudic exegesis of Rashi. We think it sounds rather strange to call the first national homecoming from exile a promenade, even if it does sound like a walk in the park compared to the second national homecoming from exile in the twentieth century. So let us imagine that the good rabbi, father or son, might have had the German/Yiddish *spazieren* in mind. Perhaps it was a spring day in Prague—or was it Jaworów in Galicia?—and as he imagined the great march from Babylon to Jerusalem, he simply felt like a short break from his dripping candle and musty desk.

Before we move on to nonmusical women, let us take a break too, with a small digression on King David.

King David was a womanizer. Not a very refined one. As a youth, victorious over Goliath, he was praised and sung by women "from all towns of Israel." As an old man, he may have had a great female poet in his bed. In between, he had quite a few wives; admittedly fewer than his son Solomon, but arguably more interesting ones.

In his book *The Same Sea,* the novelist among us lyricized David through the eyes of a young modern Israeli woman, in a chapter called "David According to Dita":

> How the day has faded. When were we talking about
>   King David,
> how did we get to talking about him? Do you
>   remember, Dita? One Friday
> night . . . you told me what it is
> about a man that attracts you: the Charles Aznavour
>   type, or Yevgeny

Yevtushenko. From them you went on to King
    David. It attracts
You when there is a needy side, a rascally side and a
    side
That plays the fool. And you also showed me from
    the balcony that night
What a ragged sexy city this Tel Aviv is.
. . . But David, you said,
reigned for thirty years in Jerusalem the ultra-
    Orthodox City of David
which he could not stand and which could not stand
    him
with his leaping and dancing and his one-night
    stands.
It would have been more fitting for him to reign in
    Tel Aviv,
to roam the city like a General (Retd.) who is both a
    grieving parent
and a well-known philanderer, a loaded high-liver
    and a king
who composes music and writes poetry and
    sometimes gives a recital,
"The Sweet Psalmist," in a fashionable venue then
    goes
off to the pub to drink with young fans and groupies.

Talmudic exegesis on King David's lifestyle is rather more
brusque. One saucy story has David refusing to marry Avishag,
because he already had eighteen wives, quite sufficient for
matrimonial bliss. Eighteen is also, incidentally, a typological

figure correlating to the Hebrew letters forming the word *alive*. Anyway, according to this Talmudic tale the persistent Avishag then mocked David, claiming that he was simply too old for the task. So David called his wife Bathsheba and—if Rav Yehuda is to be trusted—had his way with her thirteen times. This, too, is a good symbolic number in Jewish tradition.

Yet typically Talmudic, we regret to say, the story wrongs biblical women. Some of David's wives and lovers were evidently sophisticated, strong-willed, and self-serving, including the sharp-tongued princess Michal, the near-perfect Abigail (a beauty "of good brains"), and the imperious Bathsheba herself, the genetic victor, mother to Solomon.

Now let us dwell on an episode from the king's middle age. It is about the presence of God in a mixed crowd, and a certain kind of gender equality.

When David brought the Ark of the Covenant to its new abode in Jerusalem, he was overcome with joy and "danced before the lord with all his might" in scanty attire. He also handed out an equal gift of three different pastries "among all the people, among the whole multitude of Israel, from man to woman." But David's wife Michal, a king's daughter herself, was disgusted. "How honorable the king of Israel was today" she remarked sardonically, "who uncovered himself today in view of his servants' handmaids, as a good-for-nothing shamelessly uncovers himself!" Perhaps Michal was the prudish voice of ultra-Orthodox Jerusalem, as Dita of *The Same Sea* would have it. Or maybe she was just a snob.

This time, we tip our hat to the husband. The king of Israel answered his wife with great dignity and depth. It was before the lord I made merry, said David to Michal. "And I will be yet more vile than thus, and will be base in mine own sight; and with the handmaids whom you have spoken of, in their company I shall be honored!"

So much for class distinction, or classy behavior, in the ancient City of David. The author of this story finishes off, rather heavy-handedly, by telling us that Michal had no child until the day of her death. Meaning, of course, that God did not appreciate her haughty remarks, either.

But what catches the eye is David's willingness to be vile, his penchant for self-abasement in front of God, and—even more daringly—in front of the world and his wife (by which we mean the world's wife and, worse, David's wife). Many centuries later, this state of mind would become a rock of Jewish faith as well as of Jewish humor. In many ways, the ruddy king of Israel, who may have lived in the turn of the first millennium BCE, was a very Jewish Israelite. Very human, too, full of weaknesses and burning passions, blending arrogance and self-deprecation.

In this book we use the convention BCE, "before common era." But David was genuinely BC, a biological ancestor of Jesus Christ, according to the Gospels of Matthew and Luke. Jesus perhaps inherited grandpa David's gift of humility and intimacy with the divine, but not his openly sensual passions and kingly pride. They were both, however, much loved by women.

What can we make of David's "honor with the handmaids"? By no means was he a feminist. Nor was he a social leveler. His punch line is poignant precisely because handmaids were not equal even to menservants, let alone to kings. Moreover, the insistence on giving equal gifts of food to all subjects, men and women alike, may signal a uniqueness.

Usually the strong got more than the weak, and men got more than women.

Even the Bible's wonderful social laws are not based on equality. The needy widow is always a woman, the property owner obligated to her welfare is always a man. Mosaic laws are seldom gender-blind. They might stipulate what philosophers today call "distributive justice," but not of the modern matrix that aims to put all persons on an equal plain. The Bible is inegalitarian, but the lowly are to be treated with respect; they deserve justice (rather than charity), and they have voices.

Another mode of equality is tucked away in this story. Whenever a great, god-driven event takes place, men and women are in it together: singing, as we saw, and dancing, or awe-struck and dumbfounded—but together. When a biblical author wanted to tell us that something momentous was taking place, he would depict men and women rejoicing (or suffering) together. For David, making merry "before the lord" means dancing in front of men and women. Tel Aviv style. It seems that God was most present among ancient Israelites whenever the event was great enough to engage his people across all divides, sexual as well as social.

Still, a balancing statement is in order. In numerous instances in the Bible, as well as postbiblical Jewish literature, women are marginalized, silenced, cordoned off. Most of the Jewish tradition can justly be tagged chauvinist by present-day standards.

But we are looking for significant threads, not for majority attitudes. The lineages we have identified here, the Davidian strand of cross-gender peoplehood in front of God, and the Avishagian strand of assertive female voice-raising, are crucial for understanding many things Jewish, then and now.

The Bible. Not the Talmud, nor the rabbinical literature, nor any Jewish literature before the nineteenth century. The Bible is rife with powerful, active, vocal, verbal, individualized, one-of-a-kind female persons.

Numerous women are mentioned by name. To be sure, fewer than men, but those mentioned play roles in a multitude of plots with zest and aplomb. Some women actively, at times single-handedly, change Israelite history. Fact or myth, it is her-story as well as his-story, all the way from Genesis to Nehemiah. Two books, Ruth and Esther, are named after women. The Song of Songs, so we have suggested, may be narrated by a woman. The documented female Israelites are not countless, but they do require quite a bit of counting, and they certainly count.

Job's daughters spring to mind. Not the nameless three who died along with their seven brothers in the beginning of that eerie moral fable, but those born at the end of the book, emblems of divine compensation and amendment, albeit in a way alien to modern sensitivities. Seven new boys are born but left unnamed. Three girls are born and the book names them, rounding off the story: Jemima, Keziah, and Keren-happuch. Lucky girls. Not only are they put on record for posterity, not only are they reportedly pretty beyond competition, but these women also inherit on par with their brothers. "And in all the land no women were found so beautiful as the daughters of Job; and their father gave them estate among their brethren." So the happy ending, the fairytale ending of this stark morality tale, involves individual recognition and equal property rights for women. Good Job.

It gets even better in the apocryphal book *Divrei Iyov*, The Testament of Job. There the resuscitated Job divides his worldly goods among his seven sons, and when the girls complain ("Are we not your children?"), he replies that better bequests are in store for them. He presents his daughters with celestial girdles that stir "a new heart" within them, and they chant "angelic hymns" or mouth "the dialect of heavenly rulers." Their gifts, then, give rise to words of the highest order. The most beautiful line pertains to Jemima, the eldest:

> And she articulated in the language of the angels, and delivered her song to God, like the uttered songs of the angels; and the words she expressed—the wind wrote them on her dress.

And we think it is magnificent, this Way of the Wind with Words.

Biblical women come in all ages and shapes, physical and character traits. Not all of them are Israelite. Not all of them are socially prominent. Many are deeply committed to family, some are highly enterprising. They might be edgily innovative, or deeply traditional, or both at the same time. Almost all biblical women are, in some important way, agents of continuity. But continuity itself often requires a daring originality.

They do not follow the Greek pattern—either goddess or mortal heroine. They do not follow the medieval pattern—either saint or prostitute. They do not follow the European pattern—aristocracy, bourgeoisie, or lower class. They do not follow the British pattern—upstairs or downstairs—although their tents are sometimes as intricate as a manor house. The Bible's women are so variegated that they simply inhabit a full human spectrum.

Here is our parade of active women. Mind you, we have left out quite a few. We are not listing all the women in the Hebrew Bible, only some of the most interesting movers and shakers.

Eve, Mother of All that is Living. She was at the very start, but her own beginning is ambiguous. God creates her, nameless and equal to her mate, in Genesis 1, where life is blown into a male-Adam and a female-Adam together. If you don't believe us, please revisit verse 27. But then comes Genesis 2, and God creates Woman again, this time from the rib of a now-only-male Adam. In Genesis 3, after the tree and the snake, Adam names her Eve. Just as the couple is getting dressed to leave the Garden of Eden. You can tell that more than one biblical author was at work, pushing differing views on the man-and-woman equilibrium. Until one day, oh well, a tired editor must have decided, let's keep both stories and let the reader choose the best version or explain away the discrepancy.

Behind Eve's naked back hovers Lilith, a female demon inserted into the story in Talmudic times, probably by a bearded misogynist. But we will use our poetic license and insist on mentioning Lilith in our parade of biblical women. The Hebrew Bible never allowed a Lilith to whisk away all sexuality from the "proper" female protagonists. Like Eve herself, many of its strong women combine a sexual presence with powerful appetites and a brainy punch: in Eve's case, curiosity. We think that most of the Bible's great women have a Lilith in them, built into them: ambition, verve, and desire.

Sarah, matronly and manipulative. Rebecca, at first sweet and accommodating, later matronly and manipulative. Leah, unloved, sexually sophisticated, and manipulative. Rachel, beloved, sexually sophisticated, and manipulative. They make four very different matriarchs. We will not dwell on them here, but—as already mentioned—their numeric advantage over the patriarchs is interesting to us. It is not merely an aspect of ancient polygamy; these four women have personalities that cumulatively outshine their three hallowed husbands. All four are strong and pushy in their ways, but each is a world unto herself.

It may take a village to raise a child, but it takes more than one mother (or one *type* of mother) to raise a nation.

Then comes the wonderful team of Exodus. No fewer than six resourceful women brought Moses into the world and kept him there. Mother Jochebed and sister Miriam, of course. Also the midwives Shifrah and Puah, who are not on record as delivering Moses, but must have inspired his family by brazenly resisting Pharaoh's orders to kill all male Hebrew babes. The third pair are Pharaoh's daughter and her alert maid. Maternally and humanly brave, carefully planning and cleverly cooperating, this unlikely sextet outwitted bad government and brutal laws. Together they saved the boy who would become the savior of a people.

How many Jewish men have noticed, over those long millennia, that we owe the nation's greatest son and leader to the ingenuity and courage of four Hebrew and two Egyptian women? And where exactly was father Amram? Out for a drink?

We will be meeting a few other passive husbands and absentee fathers as the biblical narrative flows on. Moses himself, no stranger to fear and fleeing, fortunately grew to meet the standards set by his mother and sister. But unlike them, he took lives as well as saving lives.

Since we mention Shifrah and Puah, let us give them due credit: as midwives, they are the first female professionals ever mentioned in the Bible. They do not go on record as anyone's daughters or wives. Merely by plying their trade, they found themselves in the role of political rebels, which they performed with great panache. Commanded to kill all the male Hebrew newborns, they cheekily ignored the king's orders. Those Hebrew mothers are not like the Egyptians, Shifrah and Puah chattily informed the bloodthirsty Pharaoh; they are strong and lively, giving birth quickly, before we even show up.

Now Socrates' mother, Phaenarete, was a midwife too, in Athens of the fifth century BCE. Her name means "She who brings virtue to light," and Socrates took pride in his "noble and burly" mother. But her role in Plato's account is merely to deliver a metaphor for her son's own philosophical "art of midwifery," bringing ideas forth from men's minds.

Sail on through the book of Exodus and it is Miriam again, grown up and full of charisma: leader, prophet, singer-song-writer, the lively spirit of the twelve tribes. But let us not get too nationalistic: great non-Israelite women are marching past, leaving the deep marks of their fingernails on the skin of Jewish history. Hagar, Potiphar's wife, Zipporah (in her case it's fore-skin), Rahab, Jael, Jezebel, and—rather more gently—Ruth. We shall return to some of them. There was also the queen of Sheba, although she passes through the first book of Kings more like an exotic breeze or a public-relations agent.

Two female leaders exercising full sovereign powers are on record: Deborah the prophetess and Queen Athaliah the wicked usurper (or was she? Who can tell?). Each of these rulers has a second woman in her story, a counterpart or nemesis. Deborah won a war against the Canaanites, but the fleeing enemy general was murdered by another woman, Jael, belonging to another people, the Kenites. Though constantly on record as "Heber's wife," Jael runs the show on her own. Making the political decision to side with the triumphant Israelites, she ruthlessly kills her houseguest, Sisera, the ill-starred escapee. So Jael was both a strategist and a combatant, rather akin to Deborah herself. Poor Heber was probably in the pub.

Similarly, the evil Athaliah managed to "destroy all the seed royal" except for baby Joash, saved and hidden by princess Jehosheba. This is a bit reminiscent of the Moses story, as well as many royal chronicles of many cultures. Still, such woman-outsmarting-woman stories are relatively rare. They underscore the broad human spectrum of biblical female protagonists.

Three women are of special interest to us—Miriam, Deborah, and Hannah—because they had a way with words, expressed ideas, and changed history (also) by verbal acts. All three were in the business of mothering—a son, a brother, or a whole people. All three sang great songs of praise to the Almighty, but each of them made a significant human contribution to the feat she celebrated in verse. Miriam sang in the wake of the Red Sea crossing, Deborah following the victory over Sisera's army, and Hannah after her private triumph against her own barrenness. We sometimes associate these songstresses mainly with their respective hymns, forgetting that each was a prime actor in the events she later exalted.

Childbearing and child rearing have always been major concerns, not to say obsessions, to Jewesses all the way from matriarch Sarah to present-day career women. Consider Tamar of the book of Genesis, a dashing procreative entrepreneur if there ever was one. Tamar was the childless widow of two sickly brothers, who married her one by one according to the Israelite law of dynastic continuity. Her father-in-law, the great Yehuda, understandably refused to wed his third and last son to Tamar. Deciding to claim her right to progeny, she dressed as a streetwalker, waited on the road to Timnah, and when Yehuda showed up she seduced him incognito and became pregnant. All for a good and legal cause, from the Bible's viewpoint. It was a brilliant success, game, set, and match. Tamar rebooted the Judean lineage, mothered the whole tribe, indeed the whole Judaic kingdom, including the future King David. And Jesus Christ into the bargain, if you like.

Tamar was also a brave heart. She stood trial for her alleged whoring when her pregnancy showed, being too respectful (as even the Talmudists admiringly pointed out) to announce Yehuda the father in public. But she was also smart, cunning, and informed by a strong sense of entitlement. Lo and behold: just when she was about to be burned, Tamar sent Yehuda his own signet, cord, and staff, which she had cleverly demanded as a deposit from him when posing as a prostitute.

This is an astounding twist in an already fabulous tale. This woman, while claiming her own identity and offspring, held in her lap the insignia and the dynastic future of the greatest tribe of Israel. "She is more righteous than I!" cried the thunderstruck Yehuda. And God must have smiled too, because Tamar's smart biological start-up produced a vibrant pair of male twins.

Tamar is a standard bearer of Jewish survival and procreation against the odds. But the deep lesson, we think, is not about genetic continuance. It is about law, narrative, and the great chain of memory. It is about the signet, cord, and staff of identity. It is about cultural staying power.

Many assertive and self-conscious mothers in the Bible, as in later Jewish history, were bent not only on feeding but also on sustenance: telling and retelling the old story, teaching and reteaching the old commandments, preferably over a bowl of real food. Moral imperatives and ideas justify biological survival and make it meaningful. There are many mothering types in the Bible: those fighting to become mothers, like Sarah, Tamar, and Hannah; the midwives, Shifrah and Puah; the sisters, notably Miriam. Even the leader-prophet Deborah, possibly childless, used motherhood as her metaphor for sovereignty: "Walled towns ceased in Israel," she sang—or by a different interpretation, "Rulers ceased in Israel"—"until I, Deborah, arose; I arose a mother in Israel." It is also significant that this brilliant leader, orator, and warrior may have been named after the Bible's only other Deborah, who was the matriarch Rebecca's wet nurse.

Compare these ladies with the great female heroes of Greek mythology and theater: the goddesses are often virgins, like Athena and Artemis; they rarely mother human beings, and seldom behave in a motherly fashion. Many of them are killers. As to the tragic heroines, their tragedy ensues in dying childless, or losing their children, or even killing them. Antigone, Clytemnestra, and Medea choose death. By contrast, Israelite and Jewish female characters over the ages almost always choose life. They fare badly at times, but not in a tragic sense. Their heroism is almost invariably about surviving, rescuing, surmounting danger, and bringing babies to the world.

One awful exception was a Hasmonean-era woman, called in some sources Hannah, who allowed Antioch's troops to kill her seven sons, down to the youngest and sweetest, rather than bowing to a Greek idol, and then threw herself off the roof, or as other sources have it into the fire. This sad story is, to be sure, not the only tale of martyrdom in Jewish literature, but it is unusual in its extreme testing of motherly feelings. This woman is closer to Medea or Lady Macbeth than to most Jewish mothers, including the rough, primeval biblical brand. Most mothers evidently preferred their children to survive to tell the national stories, rather than die to become a national story. For if Jewish succession is about "living to tell the tale," then a child's life is important not only for its own obvious sake but also because the child is the precious next chapter in the book.

As to forced conversion, here is a real tragedy: the offspring of converts no longer remembers. He or she may live, but not to relay the narrative. Did any *converso* mother, as the day darkened in post-1492 Spain, ever dare to whisper to her baptized children a few words from the ancient Hebrew grace before the meal, *hu noten lechem le-khol basar*, hoping against hope that they would pass it on?

Her sister who remained Jewish, expelled to Provence or Morocco, adamantly clung to the blessed words. Witnessing countless lines of memory irretrievably broken, through the violent death or conversion of whole communities, those who remained Jews became ever stauncher in their adherence to the ancient imperative: go forth and multiply. God's words to Abraham became an engine of continuance, a double engine, for they command both remembrance and rememberers.

Who was the first "Jewish mother," *yiddishe mamme,* in history?

Beware, it is a trick question. The Jewish mother, as we know her today, is not a biblical type at all. Or, at least, her impact is somewhat subtler. Zipporah, with unmistakable convert's zeal, circumcised her son with her own hands and a sharp flintstone; some latter-day Jewish mothers use words to a comparable effect. Much has been written of this stereotype, from its guilt-ridden spike to its overloving strangulation. Yes, we know: some of the literature and the jokes are rather unkind, and some, with significant overlap, are also rather hilarious. Or else, terribly sad.

If we must choose a representative text, we'd opt for the Yiddish bard Itzik Manger, who lovingly tells his mother that by forcing him to dress very warmly, she rendered him unable to spread wings and fly. Listen to the Yiddish.

Zog ikh tsu der mame:—her,
Zolst mir nor nit shtern,
Vel ikh, mame, eyns un tsvey
Bald a foygl vern. . . .

Veynt di mame:—Itsik, kroyn,
Nem, um gotes viln,
Nem khotsh mit a shalikl,
Zolst zikh nisht farkiln. . . .

Un dos vinter-laybl nem,
Tu es on, du shoyte,
Oyb du vilst nisht zayn keyn gast
Tsvishn ale toyte . . .

Kh'hoib di fligl, s'iz mir shver,
Tsu fil, tsu fil zakhn,
Hot di mame ongeton
Dem feygele, dem shvakhn.

The English translation loses half of the original tenderness, and the Hebrew translation—three quarters. Still:

I tell the mamme: listen now,
If you don't hold me back,
I will instantly become
A bird, mamme, and fly. . . .

Cries the mamme: Itzik, gem,
In the name of God,
Take a warm *scarf'l* with you
For you may catch a cold. . . .

Take that winter-underwear
Put it on, you birdhead
Lest you want to be a guest
Among all those who're dead.

I spread a wing, but it's so heavy;
Far too many things
The mamme has piled upon
Her little weak fledgling.

Now, the spectrum of Jewish mothers "piling on far too many things" is enormous, even within the stereotype. On one extreme sits the poor and pious widow in Bialik's famous poem "My Mother, Bless Her Memory" (1931).

My mother, bless her memory, was a wholly
    righteous woman

And in widowhood, desperately poor.
Come Sabbath Eve, the sun at the treetops,
There was no candle in her home, and no meal.

She sought and found, miraculously, two pennies—
"Bread or candles?" She pondered,
Ran off and returned, a saintly burden in her thin
    hand:
The two candles for the blessing.

Then, as she lights the candles on her empty but white-clothed table, she reflects on her poverty and grief, and sheds one tear that blows a candle out. Bitterly reproaching the Lord for this mishap ("Do you spurn, God, a widow's gift?"), she finally sheds a wondrous tear that rekindles the flame.

On the other extreme, here is Alvy Singer's unsaintly mother in Woody Allen's *Annie Hall* (1977):

NINE-YEAR-OLD ALVY: The universe is expanding!
DOCTOR: The universe is expanding?
ALVY: Well, the universe is everything, and if it's expanding, someday it will break apart and that would be the end of everything!
ALVY'S MOTHER: What is that your business? [To doctor:] He stopped doing his homework!
ALVY: What's the point?
ALVY'S MOTHER: What has the universe got to do with it? You're here in Brooklyn! Brooklyn is not expanding!

Believe it or not, the saintly mother in Bialik's poem and the vulgar Mrs. Singer in Allen's film have a few things in common. Both of them would not shirk from blaming the Almighty where blame is due; and both will insist that their sons do their homework, never mind the universe. This shared interest is crucial for our story.

Bialik's pious candle lighter, by the way, was not his own mother. The poem's byline reads "From the conversations of the Righteous Man of Vilednik." That was Yisrael Dov-Ber, a Ukrainian Hasidic *tzadik* and rabbinical author of the early nineteenth century. His mother had been the widow of a primary Torah teacher, a "babies' *melamed*." Can you possibly imagine that she would *not* make her boy do his homework, just as Woody Allen's cinematic mom did in her less graceful way? By the way, the saintly widow was still Bialik's ancestor, of sorts: her son, the Righteous Man of Vilednik, was stepfather to Bialik's grandmother, who grew up in his house.

Other Jewish mothers, extremely well read themselves, offered their children a model of erudition no less than an emotional prodding to excel. We have seen Glikl of Hameln's impressive female-Jewish education, which shines through her voluminous correspondence with her children. Isaac Bashevis Singer (no relation, as far as we can determine, to Alvy) emerged from his mother Basheve's heterogeneous bookshelf no less, and arguably more, than from his father's rabbinical tomes. Marcel Proust's beloved bookish mother, Jeanne Clémence Weil, came from a refined Alsatian Jewish family. If you look at the Jewish mothers of writers and thinkers through the ages, possible patterns shine through: their love of reading might remain within the devotional sphere alone, but often enough they were more worldly, more practical, and more in touch with gentile literature or folktales, than their husbands. Agnon's mother read German stories to him. Ukrainian lore, weird, gloomy, and bewitching, passed on from Fania Klausner to her son, the novelist among us.

But let us return to our biblical candidates for the title of a primeval *yiddishe mamme*. We have two finalists. First, Hannah, wife to Elkanah, mother to Samuel (and others). Second, Bathsheba, widow of Uriah, wife to David, mother to Solomon (and others).

Both Hannah and Bathsheba would move heaven and earth for their beloved sons, and cared somewhat less about their husbands (in Bathsheba's case, the first husband got an especially raw deal). Bathsheba had the scheming, pushy motherliness of latter-day Mrs. Singer. Hannah fervently prayed for a child and promised to give him up to the service of God. And she delivered.

Both women seem to qualify. One brought her son to become high priest, the other cunningly made her son king. Perhaps these jobs are the biblical equivalents of the doctor and the lawyer. But let us announce the winner, and it is Hannah.

> And when she had weaned him, she took him up with
> her, with three bullocks, and one ephah of meal, and
> a bottle of wine, and brought him unto the house of
> the Lord in Shiloh; and the child was a child. . . .

Here is the mother of every Jewish mother who ever took her three-year-old son, his hair freshly cut, to the heder, the Hebrew schoolroom. Everywhere, from Yemen to Lithuania: give the child something good to eat and send him off to learn the alphabet. Even better, teach him the rudiments at home, if you can. Women teaching the Hebrew letters to their youngsters at the kitchen table—here was one mainstay of premodern female literacy.

The Bible gently underscores, in its terse and economic

way, almost in a fatherly way, that Samuel was really very small. At least, like Jochebed and Miriam before her, Hannah sweetened her sacrifice by watching her child grow from afar. Unlike Moses' family, she could even visit and pamper him:

> But Samuel ministered before the Lord, being a child, girded with a linen ephod. Moreover his mother made him a little coat, and brought it to him from year to year, when she came up with her husband to offer the yearly sacrifice.

Don't let the singular noun form mislead you: she made him a *new* little coat every year, fit to size, and the biblical author recognizes the sweetness of that petit priest-child clothing. For Hannah, not Bathsheba, is the earliest linchpin of the two faces of Jewish motherhood: great physical tenderness, and early scholarly sendoff. Heartbroken at the shrine or school gate, but decisively returning home to start next year's little coat.

Here, too, is the launch pad of that great Jewish twosome: bread and letters. With Hannah the food issue started earlier, when her childlessness induced a loss of appetite, to her loving husband's dismay. When the time came to fulfill her promise to the Lord (or, if you will, to Eli the priest) and bring her son to Shiloh, she also brought meat, flour, and wine. Innumerable mothers brought something tasty for the young pupil and his *melamed:* candies and pastries in Morocco and Tunisia, almonds and raisins in eastern Europe. The very first letter you read by yourself, the very first word in the very first book, was rounded by a sweet, so it was bound to taste delicious.

We think this is very wise.

Samuel's road, rather than Solomon's, is the one followed

by so many Jewish men over the ages: weaned off mother's milk, on to the synagogue-schoolroom, scrumptious almonds and raisins, aleph and bet. And Hannah's road has the heart-rending duality of so many future Jewish parents: my child is not my child alone, he belongs to God—or, even without God, to study—and I must give him up, in a deep and crucial sense, at a soft and early age.

There she stands, waving goodbye before trudging back home to the hills of Ephraim. All by herself. Though mercifully she had other children with Elkanah later on.

As centuries go by, many mothers walking home from their son's schoolroom will be able to read a little, too. But even Hannah, as you'll find if you read 1 Samuel 1 carefully, was a woman of words. She may have been illiterate—we are not told—but she coined the well-known Hebrew saying "For this child I prayed." And did you notice the smart wordplay she pulls off in verses 27–28, counterpoising the Hebrew words for *ask* and *lend*? Sorry, it's untranslatable.

In 1 Samuel 2, Hannah delivers a beautiful, poetically very refined, hymn of praise to God. Once again, we are at a loss to establish whether Hannah ever existed and who really wrote "My heart exults in the Lord." But we are fascinated by a literary culture that ascribes this polished piece of highbrow poetry to a humble woman. If ancient Israel was not truly a democracy of letters, at least its narratives often present it as such. The hymn possibly authored by Hannah is indeed about human equality before God, especially in the realm of the spoken word: "Multiply not exceeding proud talk; let not arrogancy come out of your mouth. . . . He will keep the feet of His faithful, but the wicked shall be put to silence in darkness;

for not by strength shall man prevail." But some women, like Hannah, prevailed by speaking up.

Elkanah, Samuel's father, was the best husband in the Bible. A little self-centered perhaps, as husbands occasionally are, but we owe him one of the tenderest moments in ancient literature:

"Hannah," he said, "why weepest thou? and why eatest thou not? and why is thy heart grieved? am not I better to thee than ten sons?"

No, dear, you are not. She did not answer him, at least not on record. But she duly ate, drank, and went off to the temple to pray successfully for a child.

We would like every Jewish wedding, be it observant or secular or interfaith, to include a mention of Elkanah's words to his wife, at least the first part. He was the kind of husband who saw what is going on: her face, her eating problems, her sadness. The historian among us is certain that he also noticed what she wore.

We admit that Elkanah may have missed the wife-squabbling in his own home—his other spouse Peninah teasing Hannah for being childless, and Hannah's desperate jealousy of Peninah, despite her elevated status as the beloved wife. Or, for that matter, Peninah's anguish over his clear preference. We said he was a good husband, not a perfect one.

Elkanah also allowed Hannah to fulfill her oath and decide little Samuel's fate. Like Amram, he is a rather absentee father, at least as far as the text is willing to disclose. Biblical stories tend to be sparse: they say only what they deem important. And Hannah was the important figure in Samuel's early life, just the way Jochebed and Miriam were the mainstays of baby Moses' survival. Not the father, in either case.

Still, the biblical author considered it important enough to record Elkanah's three questions. His love must have mattered, somehow.

There are other tender moments in the Bible. Naomi, who lost two sons, tells her Moabite daughters-in-law to return to their families for their own good. All three women kiss and cry, but only Ruth follows Naomi to Israel. "For whither thou goest, I will go; and where thou lodgest, I will lodge; thy people shall be my people, and thy God my God; where thou diest, will I die, and there will I be buried." This Ruth, whose story is somewhat reminiscent of Tamar's, found and married a descendant of Tamar, also related to her late husband, thus following the same legal imperative of family-lineage continuity. What we like in this story are the personal affections: Moabite to Israelite, old to young, young to old, woman to woman, and woman to man. It's not just about preserving the race. Perhaps it is not about preserving the race at all, but about being human, backtracking from disaster, and creating future hope.

Whenever the historian among us goes through the Berlin neighborhood of Moabit, Ruth springs to mind. The area carries so many other historical associations, many of them very dark, but Ruth can hold her own.

If Hannah is the harbinger of intellectual child rearing, she is certainly not the only such parent. The Woman of Valor, celebrated in the last chapter of Proverbs, is a loyal wife, caring mother, craftswoman, merchant, manager, real estate buyer, agriculturalist, almsgiver, seamstress, the pride of her male relatives, a pillar of faith, and generally a person of great success and good taste. More interesting for us, this impossibly perfect lady also "openeth her mouth with wisdom; and the Torah of kindness is on her tongue." She also gives "law to her maidens." Daughters or servants? Education or mere discipline? It is hard to say. Finally, this remarkable *eshet chail* is also an offstage politician. "Her husband is known in the gates, when he sitteth among the elders of the land." Of his own merit? Ask Amram and Elkanah.

Other women glimmer in the dark, mentioned in passing, half-forgotten, their own words lost or destroyed. But the biblical authors still allow them a peek through the curtains: Hulda the Prophetess may have deserved her own scripture, but all that is left of her on record is one prophecy of doom, repeated in two biblical books. At least we know her name, her husband's, his family pedigree, and her Jerusalem abode.

Others remain nameless, but still played big roles in important stories. Who was the Wise Woman of Tekoa, who cleverly saved Absalom's life by posing a smart parable to his father, David? Who was the Divining Woman of En-Dor, who unknowingly helped King Saul while audaciously complaining of his persecution of mystics, brought him in touch with the ghost of Samuel, scared him almost to death, and then, typically enough, made him a nice dinner?

And who was the Big Woman of Shunem, who "held" the prophet Elisha "to eat bread"? The Big Woman, also known as the Shunammite, got her husband to make a guest room for the prophet, which she meticulously designed. As you already know, biblical women blend motherly nurturing with a pinch of practical wisdom. When Elisha asked her whether she needed to make use of his political contacts, she demurely replied, "I dwell among my own people." This has become a catchphrase, in Modern Hebrew, for political and sociological astuteness. Elisha was so grateful that he took the trouble to find out that the Big Woman was childless, promised her a child, and fulfilled his promise. When her son was born, fell ill, and died, Elisha revived him. No less.

It so happens that our Avishag, David's platonic bedfellow, perhaps Solomon's emblematic lover, and perhaps even the secret author of the Song of Songs, was a Shunammite too. How is she related to the Big Woman? How is the Wise Woman of Tekoa related to the prophet Amos, from the same town? And how many other fascinating female Israelites were left in the Bible's proverbial wastepaper basket?

As Bertolt Brecht once wrote, in a somewhat comparable context: "So many reports. / So many questions."

Three big caveats are in order.

First, by no means do we suggest that other ancient societies and cultures did not raise strong, assertive, brave, wise, and vocal women. Ancient Egypt and Mesopotamia created literatures with powerful female figures. Ancient Greece and Rome had female authors and philosophers, as well as heroines historical and fictional. The very presence of several non-Israelite women in key biblical roles, as we have emphasized, proves that Midianites and Moabites, Canaanites and Kenites, Philistines and Pharaoh's daughters could turn the wheels of history just as effectively as their Hebrew peers.

But if you were a Near Eastern lady of strength and ambition, hoping to leave your stamp on the world, it certainly helped to make an entry into a biblical story. The point of our book is not that Jews were any better than others, but that Jews had a special way with words. Words became texts. The published became perennial.

We will never know how many wise women uttered wise sayings in each and every culture. But if you happened to coin the phrase "To this child I prayed," or "I dwell among my own people," or "Thy god shall be my god," you had a better chance of everlasting fame if you spoke your phrase into biblical ears. In addition, if you sent your son to the house of God or taught law to your maidens, your chances of remaining on historical record are slightly greater. By promoting the national stories, telling them and singing them to posterity, women too became part of the story.

Our second caveat refers to the "historicity" of all our biblical protagonists, male or female. We are well aware that each and every character mentioned so far might be pure fiction, a figment of some author's imagination, invented sometime between 1000 and 500 BCE. We are not assuming that Sarah, Miriam, or Hulda actually existed But *the authors existed, and their language existed.* Who inspired those stories? Where did the heroes and heroines, the plots and the fables, the dialogues and the turns of phrase, all come from? From real life, that's where. From textlines.

An archaeologist may worry that biblical accounts are mere "fiction," but we come from a different place. "Fiction" does not frighten us. As readers, we know that it conveys truths. As secular Jews, we have no stake in the historicity of Moses or Miriam. That the Storytellers were real is good enough for us. We can tell that they lived in a society well accustomed to strong, assertive mother figures. A civilization capable of writing the Bible evidently had Sarahs, Deborahs, and Huldas living in its midst. The specific ladies may have been as mythical as Greek goddesses—who cares?—but their words are the stuff of palpable human experience.

Our third caveat is simple and brusque. The Bible was not an equal opportunity employer. Women did not normally own property or inherit (with some notable exceptions). Polygamy was rife, polyandry unheard of (unless you count Michal; look her up if you are curious). Adultery was punishable by death, divorce was at the husband's whim, and fathers could sell their young daughters to slavery. "And I find the woman more bitter than death," wrote the exquisite Ecclesiastes. "One man among a thousand have I found; but a woman among all those have I not found."

We cannot understand how the sensual Song of Songs, the thoughtful book of Proverbs (with its Woman of Valor), and the sour and poetically stunning Ecclesiastes can all be ascribed to the same author, Solomon. Maybe he wrote each book under the sway of a different wife. Or maybe other people wrote them, perhaps even a wife or two.

What happened to active women during the era of the Second Temple, the Mishnah, and the Talmud?

Perhaps the story of Rabbi Akiva's wife is a good clue. According to one source her name was Rachel, but others leave her unnamed. She was a rich man's daughter; he was a humble and aging shepherd. She spotted his "excellence and modesty." If I marry you, she asked, will you go to the House of Learning? Yes, he said. They wed, her father promptly disavowed her, and Akiva went off to study. He became one of the greatest sages in Jewish history. Some versions of the story suggest that he abandoned her for many years, leaving her in abject poverty. When she finally approached him through a throng of disciples and the men tried to push her away, Akiva told them to let go of her, for "mine and yours are hers." And he bought his wife a beautiful tiara, known as "Jerusalem of Gold."

The story—gleaned from the Babylonian Talmud and other sources—has beauty. It posits Akiva's wife as a Jewish mother of sorts, sending her husband away to school at the very infancy of their marriage. But there is something unbiblical here; a victim of both father and husband, she remains behind, to be compensated by a piece of jewelry by way of happy ending. Her husband is surrounded by arrogant learned men who shun her for her sex. Despite Akiva's pretty words, the gates of the rabbinical school are firmly shut in her face.

Do not make much conversation with women, said the sages. Women are light of mind. If you teach your daughter the Torah, said Rabbi Eliezer, you are teaching her nonsense. Better burn the Torah, said Rabbi Eleazar, than give it to women. "The Torah says," wrote Josephus Flavius in *Against Apion,* "that a woman is inferior to her husband in all things." We are not aware of any place in the Torah that says quite these things. Perhaps Josephus had a different version; this is not impossible. "Let her, therefore, be obedient to him," Josephus continued, "not so that he should abuse her, but that she may acknowledge her duty to her husband; for God hath given the authority to the husband."

And so it goes.

There are dissenting opinions, too: The Mishnaic scholar ben Azzai said that a man must teach his daughter the Torah.

God gave women more understanding than men, another sage said. But the main thrust of Talmudic sexual politics is crystal clear. It affects ultra-Orthodox Judaism to this day. Its impact on Israeli and Jewish public life is still significant, even as we write these lines.

What happened?

Most Mishnaic and Talmudic scholars were working men, out-and-about men; but to pursue their study, the new oral Torah which is by definition conversational, they cloistered themselves up in their Sanhedrin, halls of learning, and synagogues, in a lettered world that shut the women out. By contrast, biblical men *and* women lived only in history, in raw, earthy, bloody history. Women thus took active part in the Bible, but they were kept at arm's length from the Talmud.

Let us offer a different historical example. Consider Europe's academic revamping in the nineteenth century. Women could run the intellectual salons of the Age of Enlightenment, engaging with Europe's brightest philosophers and writers on an equal footing. But when the hub of intellectual life shifted into the academic lecture halls of Paris, Oxford, and Berlin, those brilliant muses were left behind, languishing in their Georgian, Victorian, or Biedermeier drawing rooms until the universities allowed them in, almost a century later.

In the era of the Second Temple and the Mishnah, roughly between the sixth century BCE and the second century CE, Jews were already called Jews, their scriptures became a canon, and a great scholarly tradition developed: first oral, then written. When the Romans destroyed the Temple in 70 CE, a synagogue culture was already in bloom. And after the final, doomed rebellion in 135 CE, the already established diasporas could gradually replace Israel. The Jewish world was, by then, a men's world: bereft of political independence and homeland, but filled with scholarship and buttressed by a solid shelf of scrolls.

Women shared Jewish fate, but they could no longer partake in the carving of Jewish wisdom, pull political strings, or sing for the nation. Their words ceased, almost, to be recorded. Learning was for men. The Jerusalem Talmud says it loud and clear: does not Deuteronomy instruct, "And ye shall teach them to your sons"? Never mind that biblical Hebrew could mean "children" when it uses the all-inclusive male form. The Talmudists did not want to unearth an alternative grammar. Your sons, insists Rabbi Simon, not your daughters.

One had to be a very lucky or a very capable woman in order to be mentioned in the Talmud. Of course, female biblical figures are often discussed, and legal analyses concerning women are numerous, especially in the tractates dedicated to them. But contemporaneous women are a different story: you need just over two hands to count them.

Our stock-taking, hoping we have not overlooked anyone, includes one queen, Heleni, and the aforementioned Hannah, mother of the seven martyred sons. In several places a "matron" (*matronita*) appears, but we do not know whether this is one specific lady or a generic name for well-to-do married women, perhaps of Roman culture, who approached the rabbis with questions. Practically all other women are immediate relatives of Talmudic scholars, such as a certain Kimchit, who was lucky or virtuous enough to mother seven high priests. When the sages asked what her secret was, she ascribed her success to feminine modesty rather than intelligent mothering: "The walls of my home never saw the strands of my hair." Oh, well. At least the sages were sage enough to reply that "many have done so, and it did not work for them."

The Talmud also names several wives of sages: the wealthy widow Martha bat Boethus, who married a high priest; our aforementioned wife of Rabbi Akiva; one Judith, who mothered too many twins (a pair of daughters, Pazi and Toy, are even named), and whose husband is on record as treating her kindly despite her bitterness. Then there's Ima Shalom.

Ima Shalom is substantial. She has certain biblical qualities. Her name means Mother of Peace in Aramaic. It may have been a nickname, and if so it was well earned: she was a great Rabbi's sister and another great Rabbi's wife, and the in-laws got into a fight (of the Talmudic sort, mind you). Her pedigree, probably coupled with her wit, got her into several major stories, where she displays a range of very human traits: she mediates, she schemes, she bribes, she tends to the poor, and she worries about both husband and brother, and for good reason too, because eventually one of them indirectly causes the other's death. On that dramatic occasion, Ima Shalom said the following words of wisdom: "I have this tradition from the house of my father's father: All gates [to pleading for God's intervention] are locked, except the gates of hurt feelings."

Only two women play greater roles than Ima Shalom. Yalta, daughter of the head of the Babylonian Jewish community and wife to Rabbi Nahman, appears several times in the Babylonian Talmud. She seems to have been a true scholar and quite a character. Yalta once broke four hundred jugs of wine in a fit of rage, reportedly because a male guest did not care to let her drink from his glass; another interpretation suggests that he insulted the female sex. But she is also on record asking some very intelligent questions. Yalta found that when the Torah prohibits us from doing or consuming something, it always allows us to do or consume something rather similar. This is good analytic thinking, and the Talmudic scribes must have thought so too. On festive Sabbaths, Yalta was carried to the synagogue on a litter, an honor permitted only to great sages. She was charitable to the needy, and in particular to scholars. She reportedly taught rabbis, freely conversed with them, and sought second opinions if she didn't like what she heard.

Bruria closes our list. She is an earlier equivalent of Yalta, daughter and wife of Mishnaic sages, and also a great scholar in her own right. Her learning capacity was legendary. She won arguments. She took part in famous debates. She garnered praise for successfully polemicizing against her own father. Rabbi Joshua is on record with the rarest of compliments: "Well said Bruria!" She had students, and her own pedagogic ways: one day she kicked a lad who whispered his lessons, telling him that only with loud oral reading can one memorize the text. Kicking apart, we challenge modern schools to take heed. Bruria also taught her husband to pray for the repentance of the wicked, not for their demise.

And late-Talmudic reports claim Bruria lay tefillin, a male-only rite of sanctity. The sixteenth-century kabbalist known as the Holy Ari, Rabbi Isaac Luria Ben Shlomo, explained that Bruria's soul came "from the world of males." She must have been an exceptional genius to pass through all those walls.

But when Rabbi Jose asked Bruria, "Which way to Lod?" she scolded him. A four-word question is an extravagance when two would suffice: "Which Lod?" Bruria, a sage in her own right, thus reproached a fellow savant for making excessive small talk with a woman, the woman being herself. Didn't the rabbis instruct not to indulge in much conversation with females? Poor Bruria. If the story is true, she suffered what critical scholars today call "internalized inferiority."

And that's about it.

The Talmud had a deep impact on the fate of future generations of Jewish women. In some neighborhoods of Jerusalem, Bnei Brak, and Brooklyn, it still does.

But it could not render them voiceless forever. Throughout the Diaspora—by which we mean diasporic space and diasporic time—being Jewish depended on spoken words, and increasingly on written texts. Women have no inferiority when it comes to words. Even the Talmud conceded that "ten measures of speech descended to the world, and the women took nine." If this is meant to be an insult, it is working the opposite way.

Premodern Jewish communities, everywhere, kept women at home and at bay. As Rachel Elior put it, "Women . . . occupied a secondary position—socially inferior, denied a public voice, excluded from the circle of scholars, maintained in ignorance, and legally discriminated against—for they were regarded as periodically impure by reason of their menstrual cycles, which excluded them from holiness and study." Isolated, marginalized, often illiterate, and in a deep sense speechless: Jewish women in premodern time did not fare much better than almost all other women on the globe.

And yet, by the late Middle Ages, both social status and erudition were on the rise in several diasporas. More women had access to letters, and left written testimonies of various kinds. Among post-1492 Sephardi communities, many women were literate. In central and eastern Europe, too, their status improved compared to Talmudic standards.

For a long time they could not approach the books, because books were expensive, and mostly kept in synagogues, houses of learning, and other male sanctuaries. So the history of Jewish women is closely tied with the material history of books. When books could finally become domesticized, kept in the family home, three great changes began to occur: in the content and rituals of the family home, in the character and genres of books, and in the women, who were finally granted proximity to written words. In several parts of Europe books gradually became more available and more affordable, thus entering more houses, even before Rabbi Gutenberg of Mainz, and increasingly after him.

Think of small candles gradually lit up and down the broad map of Jewish dispersal. In Baghdad, North Africa, Spain, Provence, Italy, France, and on to central and eastern Europe, reading lights came on for some women. We imagine the parlors of the well-to-do, the wives and daughters of rabbis and authors, dignitaries and merchants, slowly gaining access to the parchments and codices. And soon enough, the reading lights became writing lights too.

An exquisite and little-known female voice emerges from the Cairo Geniza, a trove of Hebrew manuscripts tucked away in the attic of the Ben Ezra Synagogue of Fustat, Old Cairo, and accidentally discovered in the late nineteenth century. It held hundreds of thousands of scrolls and parchments, books and fragments, texts hitherto deemed lost or never known, authored by the Heads of the Babylonian Diaspora (Exilarchs), late-antiquity and medieval scholars, and Sephardi poets. Quite a few documents—letters, wills, and petitions—may have been written or dictated by women. And one little scrap of rag paper, torn in half, carries a unique text: a short and gorgeous love poem in Hebrew, to a husband far away:

> Will her love remember his graceful doe,
>> her only son in her arms as he parted?
> On her left hand he placed a ring from his right,
>> on his wrist she placed her bracelet.
> As a keepsake she took his mantle from him,
>> and he in turn took hers from her.
> Would he settle, now, in the Land of Spain
>> if its prince gave him half his kingdom?

We salute the English translators of this poem, but the Hebrew original is stand-alone splendid. The author should have become a great poet. We do not even know her name.

Her identity was established thanks to the textual detective work of the Israeli scholar Ezra Fleischer. If his hypothesis is correct, the tiny fragment of paper with part of this poem under the inscription "Of [which can also mean 'to'] the spouse of Dunash Ben Labrat" reveals a female authorship. We know nothing of that tenth-century woman. Her husband was the great harbinger of the Sephardi golden age, the first to write profane poetry alongside devotional verse. How many other torn fragments, in female hands, were lost to posterity?

We imagine them learning to read at kitchen tables, by the stoves, or huddled in the corner of a learned father's room. Some fathers must have called their smart girls to their desks, in order to teach, read, and argue. We imagine a father painfully turning his gaze from a slow son to his bright sister. Or a literate mother passing the torch to her girls, "giving law to her maidens."

Rashi's three daughters are a case in point. That shining beacon of biblical and Talmudic exegesis, Rabbi Shlomo Yitzhaki by his full name, had no sons. In dark eleventh-century France—and dark and dismal it was, with the First Crusade massacring many thousands of Jews, and general female literacy near zero—Rashi taught his girls Torah and Gemarah. At least two of them were reportedly very bright. Their names were Jochebed, Miriam, and Rachel. Their scholarly husbands, and even more scholarly sons, joined Rashi in creating a new school of thought and interpretation. This brainy clan somehow survived the Crusaders, and its genealogy of wisdom prevailed.

And so they march up the centuries, the learned Jewish women. Scholars and writers, merchants and intellectuals. Sephardi and Ashkenazi, married or single, some blessed with inspiring fathers, some becoming inspiring mothers. At first they are few and far between, then they are many. Enter Dulcea of Worms and Licoricia of Winchester, twelfth-century Jewish women with pens. In Italy, wives and daughters of Jewish printers became publishers, scribes, and authors in their own right. Strong Sephardi matrons mongered political power and made names and voices for themselves: Benvenida Abravanel hails from the fifteenth century, Dona Gracia Nasi and Devorà Ascarelli from the sixteenth. In Kurdistan, Osnat Barazani was as great a rabbi as her father and grandfather. Perhaps greater. We have already met the awe-inspiring Glikl of Hameln. The eighteenth century brought Frekha Bat Yosef, Moroccan poet and prayer writer. Rachel Morpurgo, in the nineteenth century, wrote religious and secular verse eventually published as *Rachel's Harp.*

The ancient art of female conversation—mentioned and

derided by the Talmud—waxed truly brilliant with the *salon-nières* of the Berlin Enlightenment, Dorothea Mendelssohn-Schlegel, Rahel Varnhagen, and Henriette Herz. They were charming and sophisticated, at home among scientists, philosophers, and Romantic writers, fascinating and outwitting them, occasionally marrying them. A few decades later, daughter to a self-made Paris muse and an unknown father, Sarah Bernhardt dazzled the French stage and made her way to early cinema.

And almost at the same time, across the continent in ultra-Orthodox eastern Europe, Hannah Rachel Verbermacher, the Maiden of Ludmir, let her great genius outshine and shame Hasidic patriarchy. She became a true-to-form *rebbe* with a circle of students around her, despite fierce opposition, until they married her off, hoping to silence her. And still she spread her wings, making her way to Jerusalem, and by some reports teaching a flock of loyal disciples there until her death.

Yes, Jewish women were often silenced, like almost all other women in all other cultures till modern times. Those we know, those we have listed, are tiny bright specks on a large dark canvas, where millions of people reside that we shall never hear from.

Osnat Barazani, that other Jewess who earned the title of rabbi against all odds, shining through male-written history by the sheer power of her intellect, in seventeenth-century Mosul, gives an inkling of that staunch, minimalist survival of Jews and words. One report has it that Osnat begged the Lord to close her womb, so that she could dedicate all her energy to study—but only after she gave birth to a son and a daughter. And another story relates that her synagogue burnt to the ground, but only after Osnat uttered some magic spell, and the holy books survived unscathed. Here you have them, once again: the children and the books. The bare bones of continuity.

The nineteenth century and the early twentieth century were a Time of Gifts for many Jewish women. All over Europe, some still in traditional attire and certainly in traditional households, they were avidly obtaining books and reading, reading with great thirst, and paving the way for their daughters and granddaughters. Not only the holy scriptures anymore, not only religious compilations for female readers like *Tzena urena*, but novels and poems and history and geography, science and practical guides and modern languages. By the late nineteenth century, as Iris Parush argues, Jewish women may have been the most enthusiastic readers in Europe.

Even when they lived very traditional lives, these women could now streamline their wisdom to great effect. Isaac Bashevis Singer's beautiful family memoir, *In My Father's Court*, has his highly intelligent and widely read mother piously serving his devout father, who only had eyes for the Talmud. The father never looked at a woman, and would not offer as much as a chair to female litigants who came to his home for rabbinical adjudication. But a paternal great-grandmother, Hinde Esther, was so admired for her wisdom and piety that Rabbi Shalom of Belz himself would seat her at his *tisch*—the all-male table of learning—whenever she came to see him. Hinde Esther even wore the male-only prayer shawl. Such was the complex spectrum on which cerebral Jewish women lived, on the threshold of modernity, but still indoors, as new promises flickered outside.

In Hamburg, Miriam Cohn, wife to Rabbi Joseph, ran his rabbinical office and adjudicated between rivals in his stead, fearlessly criticized his teachings, and took a crucial part in the daily Torah lessons of their grandson. Miriam was certainly not the only or the best-known *rebbetzen* to out-Rabbi her own husband. But that grandson of hers happened to become Israeli Supreme Court Justice Haim Cohn. "She is the one who taught me," Cohn reminisced, "that no truth is absolute, and that independence of mind must never be compromised."

What other traditional society, one wonders, produced so many documented, named, vocal, and opinionated female members *before* the onset of modernity?

By the early nineteenth century, still excluded from most halls of learning, there were many more Brurias, Yaltas, and Ima Shaloms to come knocking on the doors of education. And so, by the time universities opened their long-shut gates to both Jews and women, they were more than ready.

It did not take two generations, not even one. Right away, immediately, Jewish women rose to the academic fore, as far as they were permitted. The chemist and physicist Elsa Neumann, the first woman to receive a doctoral degree at the University of Berlin (in 1899), nine years before women were officially allowed to study. Lise Meitner, the second woman to receive a Ph.D. in physics from the University of Vienna, and in many opinions well meriting a Nobel Prize. The bacteriologist Lydia Rabinowitsch-Kempner in Bern. The political philosopher Simone Weil. Hannah Arendt, who shone in Königsberg and Marburg and Heidelberg. Also in Heidelberg, the medical scholar Rahel Goitein Straus and the historian Selma Stern. German and Austrian Jews were the earliest pioneers of this female breakthrough in the sciences; many followed suit, including the British biophysicist Rosalind Franklin. No doubt we must apologize for numerous omissions. If Talmudic women can be counted on two hands, their modern counterparts require hundreds.

When our great- (and great-great-) uncle Joseph Klausner arrived in Heidelberg in 1897, he thought he was in heaven. There was such marvelous intellectual company over many a mug of beer in the *Kneipe* after the philosophical seminar. There were so many clever women. And so many of them Jewish. Not that Klausner minded if they were not.

The years of German-Jewish flourishing ended abruptly and brutally. When Hitler's Germany tried to wipe out every Jewish life and silence every Jewish voice, gender was no divider. Of the millions of throttled voices, half were female. An equal half.

Today's Miriams no longer rely on their brothers, nor Brurias on their husbands, nor Osnat Barazanis on their fathers. The Jews no longer have any reading advantage over other nations and cultures. Powerful female voices are everywhere, almost everywhere, a fact of human life.

Our winding narrative of inclusion and exclusion, of strong and silenced voices, is not only about Jewish women. It can also read as an all-human fable of survival-by-remembrance. The dozens of protagonists linked together in this chapter form not a genetic continuum, but rather a series of people carrying texts, burdened with ideas, stubbornly and lovingly passing them on to flesh-and-blood children along with their milk and bread. We shall never know whether Yalta descended from Sarah, or whether the Maiden of Ludmir carries Yalta's genes? What matters is that Yalta read about Sarah, and that Hannah Rachel Verbermacher studied Yalta. It was not about the biological father but about the continuance of the story. The legacy of identity. The textual equivalents of Yehuda's signet, cords, and staff.

And, of course, the child who will carry them into the future. Ask Tamar. She understood.

THREE

Time and Timelessness

JEWS HAVE BEEN interested in time since time immemorial.

All civilizations are deeply concerned with their pasts: this, among other things, is what makes them into civilizations. So biblical narratives and Talmudic tales, rabbinic discussions and Sephardic poetry, Jewish Enlightenment works and Hasidic lore, and modern scholarship and literature display a cumulative wealth that is no different from, though arguably a bit more spread out than, other cultural genealogies.

The Hebrew creation stories, our "In the Beginning," the first family, our antediluvian and postdiluvian tales, the Flood itself—are in many ways akin to Babylonian, Assyrian, and Greek myths. Monotheism may be our particular spice, but the dish is universal. And Genesis is not even that monotheistic: all manner of primordial deities and vanquished demons crawl through the text. Who was Tehom, appearing as early as Genesis 1:2, and conventionally understood as "abyss" or "The Deep"? She is suspiciously reminiscent of the Babylonian

Tiamat, goddess of chaos and sea. Is Tehom the fossil of a pagan deity, still powerful enough to creep into the Bible? Who were the Great Sea Monsters brought to life on the fifth day of creation, and why are they singled out among God's other creatures? Who was Leviathan?

Ah, Leviathan. The gigantic arouser of vivid imagery, from Thomas Hobbes through Herman Melville to *Pirates of the Caribbean*. Those dark and distressing lines from the Book of Job must have shaken many a childish mind: "Lo, let that night be desolate; let no joy come therein. Let the cursers of the day bedamn him, who are set to awaken Leviathan." Lo, the imaginings in the reading child's mind! Little Isaac Bashevis Singer, sauntering out of the crowded streets of Warsaw for the first time in his life, off with his streetwise friend Boruch-Dovid to the river's green banks.

> "That's the Vistula," explained Boruch-Dovid. "It flows all the way to Danzig."
> "And then?"
> "Then it flows into the sea."
> "And where is the Leviathan?"
> "Far away, at the end of the earth."
> Then the storybooks did not tell lies, after all.
> The world *is* filled with wonders.

The wonders, for Isaac, though perhaps not for Boruch-Dovid, were all born in the books. Only later were they imprinted onto real life, prompted by the recollection of words, awakened by the Leviathan of textual marvel.

Of several great scholars who have informed our biblical reading over the years, the historian among us fondly recalls reading Umberto (Moshe David) Cassuto and Yehezkel Kaufmann. They taught us to look for pagan, idolatrous, mythical remnants under the Bible's tight monotheistic corset. Their scholarship flowed enticingly into our secular Bible classes. They showed us that criticism can be delicious.

All this is to say that the Jewish past is closely knitted with other peoples' pasts. By the time Josephus Flavius, born Yosef ben Matitiyahu, wrote his histories of the Jews in Greek in the first century CE, it was clear that all histories constantly cross paths. You have to be a diehard cultural separatist to ignore the universal themes. "A people that shall dwell alone, and shall not be reckoned among the nations"? Come now, Balaam. There was constant mutual reckoning. The uniquenesses and peculiarities of Jewish history are precisely what brought Jews in touch with so many other peoples, cultures, and ideas.

We are a nation with far more history than geography. Like a primeval Forrest Gump we seem to crop up uncannily in every important juncture in the annals of the Middle East and Europe. Our names, words, concepts, and ideas resurface everywhere today. There are Bethlehems in America, Moabites in Berlin, and Rebeccas in Hong Kong. We seem to have touched everything. And yet, for many centuries many Jews remained outside of history, by their own lights. Diaspora rabbis of a messianic bent, who identified the end of the Jewish exile with the end of time itself, spent their lives expecting Last Summons to sound any day now. Jews in some places were buried holding twigs, to dig their way underground to Jerusalem when the Messiah blows his horn. Today, too, some Jews purport to live by their collective inner chronometer alone. Many others were subjected to a rude awakening, as twentieth-century history invaded and destroyed their Jewish time. Zionism, Marxism, secularism, modern life, death by the Waffen SS.

Some Jewish dealings with time we find brilliant and bizarre. There are moments when Grandpa Clock himself seems to riot, twist, and pirouette. Consider two truly timeless Jews, the prophet Zechariah and Albert Einstein. Zechariah foresaw a day coming near, only God knows when, which shall be "neither day nor night," both evening and noon, both summer and winter. Albert Einstein, for his part, changed our grasp of time by incorporating it as a factor in his special theory of relativity, and quipped: "The only reason for time is so that everything doesn't happen at once."

We would not delve here into Einstein's interplay of time and space even if we could, because we do not see the special theory of relativity as particularly Jewish (except in its sheer chutzpah). Instead, we invite you to dwell on the biblical sense of holiness. You may be surprised to learn that there is no "holy land" in the Bible, and the only sacrosanct place is the Temple in Jerusalem, God's Holy Mountain. However, there are many "holy times." In the holy days the whole people—regardless of rank or gender—were invited to partake in "holy reading." In the Talmud the Hebrew language, no longer in everyday use, became the "holy tongue." Thus, when the Jews lost Jerusalem and its Holy Mountain, they could still carry with them into the bitter Diaspora their nonspatial, intangible holies: the language, the readings, and the ever-recurring, cyclically comforting calendar of "holy times."

Not that Jews ever had one solid philosophy of time. They

have several. For example, time could assume a circular shape. Ecclesiastes put it best:

> That which hath been is that which shall be, and that which hath been done is that which shall be done; and there is nothing new under the sun. Is there a thing whereof it is said: "See, this is new"?—It hath been already, in the ages that were before us. There is no remembrance of those that came first; neither shall be any remembrance of those that will come last.

Very sobering, yes. However, Ecclesiastes' enchanting ennui did not preclude him from toiling on his poetry. His singular art shines through those verses, telling us, "See, this is new!" We are certain that this author—Solomon by tradition, although his Hebrew vocabulary attests to a later era—had a poetic ego, and expected posterity to remember him. They did. Most deservedly.

You may want to know why we think Ecclesiastes was male. If the Song of Songs might have a female author, why not the next book on the biblical shelf? Well, call it veteran reader's intuition, but we wager this is a male text. The languor and world-weariness, the luxurious despair coupled with blasé entitlement, are masculine, and rather aristocratic. It might well be Solomon himself.

But Ecclesiastes' sense that time is meaningless was not at all typical of Israelite writers before him or Jewish writers after him. We think that it is still out of character today. Even the Viennese therapist Viktor Frankl, surviving Theresienstadt and Auschwitz, having lost almost everyone he loved, still had more use for the word *hope* than *despair* in his *Man's Search for Meaning* (1946). Likewise, Mischa, in Jurek Becker's *Jakob the Liar*, tells himself and fellow ghetto inmates, "It does make sense to speak of the future." The Holocaust did not produce a latter-day Ecclesiastes. Suicides, yes. Individuals who lost the battle for meaning, yes. But no one wrote, after Auschwitz, anything akin to "there is nothing new under the sun." Somehow, the circularity or repetitiveness of history was no longer an option.

So let us consider linearity. There is a modern, post-Enlightenment linearity that our contemporaries easily recognize. We are progressing toward a glorious future, or rushing toward a dismal man-made catastrophe, or (less likely, it currently seems) moving onto an even, everlasting, end-of-history plateau. These are three sides of the same modern coin. It is a secular linearity, for better or worse, coming from an all-human past, and leading to a future instigated by us. There are no otherworldly terminals.

Mythical or religious linearity is a different story. Its beginning and end are ethereal. Ancient Greece had myths of a simple early human existence (later authors associated it with Arcadia), and a sweet afterlife realm, the termination of time, Elysium. We might think that there are clear Hebraic equivalents. Does not the Garden in Eden match the first, and Isaiah's "end of days" parallel the latter?

Well, Eden of the book of Genesis is arguably comparable to other myths about the beginning of human time. But the Jewish final station is more questionable. What Isaiah had in mind, when speaking of "the end of days," is not a Greek

Elysium, much less a Christian Second Coming, or Armageddon, or the Last Judgment. Isaiah's vision takes place on earth, politics is still meaningful, and life is still physical.

We cannot resist a digression on Armageddon.

Saint John the Evangelist identified Mount Megiddo as the scene of the Last Battle between Satan and God. Armageddon derives from the Greek form of the Hebrew *Har Megiddo*. This is a clear geographic pointer, part of the Carmel mountain range. Megiddo happens to be one of the region's earliest known settlements, dating back to neolithic times. Over the millennia it was an Egyptian taxpaying domain, a Canaanite stronghold, and an Israelite walled city. In the valley below, in 609 BCE, the king of Egypt defeated and killed Josiah, king of Judea. Today it is a well-kept archaeological park.

In their challenging book *The Bible Unearthed: Archaeology's New Vision of Ancient Israel and the Origin of Its Sacred Texts*, two archeologists whom we have already mentioned, Israel Finkelstein and Neil Asher Silberman, argue that scientific findings increasingly contradict biblical narrative, or at least do not substantiate it. David and Solomon lorded over a poor and politically insignificant realm. Jerusalem was a large village. The early kingdom of Judea left us few material remains, and what's left is dismally meager. Here is the unsentimental bottom line: David and Solomon, their cities and their glory, were all hyped up by later kings and their nimble chroniclers. Those latter-day monarchs, members of the Omride dynasty, fabricated and lionized the crude Davidian past for their own ends. Call it pious fiction or public relations. Spin.

Megiddo, too, say Finkelstein and Silberman, was not

Solomon's grand city as previous archeologists, bowing to biblical convention, took for granted. It was fortified by the Omride kings but had little to boast in earlier eras. Our great biblical narrative of Saul, David, and Solomon—not to mention all figures who allegedly preceded them—is an even later construct, concocted from old tales by the scribes of the same King Josiah who perished in the Megiddo Valley.

Finkelstein and Silberman's book is considered provocative. Some archeologists share similar observations, while other scholars claim that the biblical stories are far too sophisticated and urban to have been crafted in the coarse environment these authors suggest. Moreover, many readers, like us, refuse to be shocked. Our Bible is made of intricate texts, not disappointing excavations. "Literature and historiography," writes Rachel Elior, "document linguistic, historical and cultural layers far more clearly and accurately, depicting the writers' world far better than piles of stones, whose vagueness is not concretely decipherable."

In a vibrant public debate that began even before the publication of *The Bible Unearthed,* Israel's greatest songwriter-poet, Naomi Shemer, memorably snapped, "I am no specialist in archaeology, but who cares whether it happened or not? Suppose the Bible never was, but was only a fable; I think this fable is more alive than all the stones."

We, for our part, do care, and would love to know "whether it happened or not" if only we could. The Bible, for us, is a tricky cocktail of fact, myth, and the sort of fiction that can convey deep truths. But we heartily agree with Shemer on her fundamental point. The grandeur of ancient Israel is not a matter of cities and kings. Material life may well have been crude, buildings rough-hewn, and clothing coarse. Solomon's splendid palace may well be a flimsy abode, a fib, or a fable. In all honesty, ancient Jewish architecture is not a major point of pride.

But the texts are palatial.

Genesis, Isaiah, and Proverbs are our pyramids, our Chinese Wall, our Gothic cathedrals. They stand undemolished in the flow of time. They have fed a plethora of offspring: from Mishnah to Haskalah, from medieval Sephardic poetry to Modern Hebrew literature, from Gotthold Ephraim Lessing to William Faulkner, all were able to drink from those deep wells.

This book is not about current affairs. We are not bringing our take on Jewish history and continuity to bear on the present-day Israeli-Palestinian conflict. But we cannot ignore the political meaning of our claim to a Jewish textline, and our belief in the superiority of books over material remains. Our sense of a Jewish history, which indeed springs from the Bible, does not need the Bible to stand for God's own word. Nor do we require it to be "historically accurate." Far be it from us to use the scriptures to stake a Jewish claim to the full expanse of Solomon's legendary empire, and to every ancient stone therein. Nor do we have any ideological use for the biblical Jerusalem to be a glorious city of great edifices. Our inheritance is compiled of a few modest geographical markers and a great bookshelf.

We will happily share our hazy, shimmering biblical geography with our Palestinian neighbors, if they too give up some of their past for the sake of a future. As to the books, there was never a question of keeping them to ourselves.

Now back to Megiddo.

Today it is a kibbutz, founded by Holocaust survivors and former partisans, perched at the foot of the large archeological site. Busloads of tourists arrive to see what's become of Armageddon. But for generations of Israelis raised on Hebrew children's literature, the name strikes a totally different chord. It belongs to the first line of a beloved book by poet Leah Goldberg, the closest thing we have to a classical nursery rhyme:

> Pluto is a puppy from Kibbutz Megiddo.
> He's got everything: some stew and a bone.
> It's all very nice, but the bone of the matter's
> He is tired of sitting here all alone.

This is what words do: they play tricks on us. If the infant listener and the child-reader can already sense that "bone" means two different things in this verse, further layers of double entendre will emerge to adult eyes. Words generate different meanings in different ears, eras, cultures, and languages. Your Armageddon is my Kibbutz Megiddo. The home of Goldberg's Pluto the Pup is the field of Saint John's Last Battle with the Antichrist. My early childhood rhyme is your apocalyptic end of time. And this is one of many reasons why we love words.

Isaiah and Micah spoke of "the end of days." Daniel mentioned the mysterious "end of wonders." Note that these expressions denote time, not place. They are neither Paradise nor Elysium. The "end" will be part of human history. It is a future era of bliss, but corporeal bliss, political even, with food and homes and cities and peace. Daniel, a mystic, says that the dead will awaken and the just will be rewarded. But the political-minded Isaiah and Micah are more interested in international relations. Many nations will come up to Jerusalem, and heed Israel's God, and cease practicing war. The physical world and its variegated peoples will continue to exist. Folk will still raise crops, enjoy sensual pleasures, and treat their neighbors kindly.

Elsewhere in the Bible "the end of days" denotes a distant but historical future, as in Jacob's seminal speech to his twelve sons. There is a smooth continuity between the language of real life and the language of promised divine bliss. The same goes for that idyllic image, "every man under his vine and under his fig tree." In 1 Kings, 2 Kings, and Isaiah, this phrase, with small variations, refers either to a past historical period or to the near future, as a political promise. But in Micah it is part of "the end of days." So yes: even then, there will be vines and figs to sit under. There will be private ownership of those vines and figs. However, *everyone* will own a vine and a fig tree. We will all eat and drink and never fear.

Centuries later, rabbinic and Midrashic sources came under the influence of pagan and Christian eschatology, creating a blurry Jewish notion of a Day of Judgment and unworldly eternal bliss. But there's a twist: even in that vague Jewish paradise, out of this world, food and drink must still be served. Without food, how can one seriously be studying the Torah for all eternity? So the Jewish table is set with both books and delicacies even in afterlife.

One version depicts a great everlasting banquet. It is for just men, and it is just for men. The Righteous will feast on the flesh of Leviathan and Wild Ox (also dubbed Behemoth), and drink "preserved wine." The Gemarah says God himself will serve up the feast, cooked from the vanquished monsters after they gore one another. Hasidic lore is happy to repeat the story, but adds that Leviathan and Behemoth also represent two types of intellect: ethereal and earthy. In Haim Be'er's novel *Back from Heavenly Lack,* the author—raised in an Orthodox Jerusalem family and familiar with every nook and cranny of Jewish textdom—plays wonderful interpretative games with this story.

But the wives of those feasting just men, in good Talmudic fashion, are not at the table. They are the footrests at their husbands' feet. Literally. At least they don't have to cook the meal.

And this reminds us of a little gem by Isaac Leib Peretz, *Sholem Bayis* (Domestic bliss). Hailing from late-nineteenth-century Poland, it is the story of a simple porter and his wife, Haim and Hannah, who are poor, content, and deeply in love. He is probably illiterate, but goes to the schoolroom every Sabbath to "hear the Torah." She cannot afford to buy enough food, but "cooks like an angel" and knows the Sabbath prayer by heart. The oldest boy studies at the heder. Let Tolstoy turn in his grave! This fine story is about a happy family.

Except that Haim worries whether he will merit eternal bliss.

> And once, after the study, he came up to the *melamed* and said:
>
> Rabbi!—And his voice trembles very much—Rabbi, how can I merit an afterlife?
>
> . . . —Every evening, bring the Torah students in the schoolroom cold water to drink.
>
> Haim's face beamed with joy.
>
> —And I will merit an afterlife?
>
> —With God's mercy.
>
> —Rabbi, Haim kept asking, and my wife?

The *melamed* told him that the husband merits on behalf of his wife, and when he sits on his chair in the Garden of Eden, his wife is his footrest.

—

Haim returned home to make *havdalah* on the wineglass, and Hannah sat and prayed "God of Abraham."

And Haim told her what the *melamed* said, but as he spoke he was suddenly filled with pity for her, and exclaimed:

—And I tell you, Hannah, that I don't want this! I will never agree for you to be my footrest—I will lift you up and seat you on my right-hand side, and we will sit together! There's enough room for us on one chair! And I am sure—he bravely added—that the Holy One, blessed be his name, would agree to it, of course he would agree, **against his will** he would agree.

The emphasis is in the original. What a telling little story "Domestic Bliss" is. In microcosm, it contains almost every theme expounded in the present book: family and study, food and text, gender gaps and rebellion against them, times past and the timeless hereafter, alongside gritty workaday life. It has that persistent admixture of reverence and irreverence that singles out the best Jewish texts. It even includes that rare but recurring moment when God is told, with all due respect, to let us handle it ourselves.

Jewish sources do not habitually spend much time on the end of time. We have shown how "the end of days" can be read in the temporal sense, a distant earthly prospect. The return from diaspora forecast by Jeremiah and the attack of Gog prophesied by Ezekiel also occur within political history.

But the Jewish take on linear time is not the modern march of history. The prominent Enlightenment paradigm of progress sees time as an arrow shot from the past to the future. The modern mind "looks ahead" or "looks forward" to the days to come, "progresses" to better times, and "harks back" to eras past.

The Hebrew language suggests something tantalizingly different. When we speak Hebrew, we literally stand in flow of time with our backs to the future and our faces toward the past. Our very *posture* is different from the Western view of time.

We owe this astounding insight to the modern Talmudic scholar Rabbi Adin Steinsaltz, further pursued by the author and essayist Shulamith Hareven in her brilliant essay "Language as Midrash." "Steinsaltz once defined Jewish time as if the Hebrew speaker stands on the bank of a river, looking upstream, against the current," she writes. The Hebrew word *kedem* means "ancient times," but the derivative *kadima* means "frontward" or "forward." The Hebrew speaker literally looks frontward to the past.

Likewise, *lefanim* is "a long time ago" but also "in front," or literally "to the face." Similarly, Hareven points out that *achareinu* means "after us" in two senses: "behind us" and "in future." Indeed, consider the biblical "end of days" we have just discussed, *achrit ha-yamim*. Like the aforementioned *achareinu*, Isaiah and Micah's *achrit* derives from *achor*, backward.

For the record: *achor* also means backside, as in that lovable Talmudic quip, "The backside of a lion is better than the backside of a woman." But we are not going there.

If Rabbi Steinsaltz saw us Hebrew-speakers standing by

the river of time and looking upstream, the present authors prefer to imagine us swimming in that river, along with the current to be sure, but legs first, and faces turned back to the faraway first fountainhead.

Is this a reactionary stance? In a sense, yes. Some Jews living today are indeed past-regarding in ways that other Jews, like us, deem restrictive and debilitating.

But in another sense, this Jewish backward-gazing forward march is a metaphor for human life in general. To pick a modern image we once heard, but can't remember where: life is like driving a car with its front window opaque. All you have to go by are your rearview mirrors. This is how we are all destined to drive.

There is some merit to moving in history with an eye on your past. Be informed and selective; know the stories and decide for yourself what is proudly displayed in the living room and what gathers dust in the basement. Let bygones be bygones and let relevancies reemerge.

The *kedem* etymological family offers an intriguing case in point. *Kedem* means not only "ancient times" but also "east." In fact, it is likely that "east" was the earliest meaning. It may have referred to Abraham's Mesopotamian origin. Now scholars have long associated Eden with Mesopotamia: you will remember that God put Adam, and subsequently created Eve from his rib, in "a garden eastward in Eden," *gan be'eden mikedem,* watered by four rivers including the Tigris and the Euphrates. One generation later, after murdering Abel, Cain "dwelt in land of Nod, on the east of Eden."

Even more telling is the word *kadima,* a derivative of *kedem.* It means "eastward" in the Bible, "ahead of" or "preceding" in the Talmud, and "onward" in Modern Hebrew.

Much as the word denotes progress today, inspired by the Yiddish-modernist term *forwerts* (פֿאָרווערטס), its ancient usage points in the opposite past-looking direction.

For Diaspora Jews, the East was no longer Mesopotamia but Jerusalem. This was not geographically fair to the Jews of Babylon—modern Iraq—or to the Persian, Yemenite, and Indian communities. But it fitted those in Europe and North Africa. Three times a day men pray toward Jerusalem, and each synagogue has an Eastern Wall. So every observant Jew did, and still does, literally look frontward, eastward, and to the distant past, all at the same time. All in one word.

Such multiple meanings make *kadima* comparable to the word *orient,* of Latin origin, denoting rise (as in sunrise), east, and direction. But *kadima*'s blend is even richer, because it involves both progress and antiquity, making it one of the single most powerful words in the lexicon of modern Jewish homecoming.

When the Zionist movement awakened Hebrew from its bookish slumber, new and exciting usages came up. Most famously, the first two stanzas of Naphtali Herz Imber's stirring poem *Tikvatenu* (Galicia, 1878). These stanzas were later renamed *Hatikvah* (The hope) and made into the Israeli national anthem. Here is an English translation of the original, which was only slightly changed in the later version:

> As long as in the heart, within,
> A Jewish soul still yearns,
> And onward (*kadima*), towards the edge of East,
> An eye to Zion gazes,
>
> Our hope is not yet lost,
> The ancient hope

To return to the land of our fathers
The city where David encamped.

East and Ancient are still there, but the forward-looking
meaning of *kedem* becomes the prevalent one in Zionist thinking. Its vision was new, indeed revolutionary: no divine redemption, no collective arising from the dead at the gates of
Jerusalem, but a human reclaiming of the biblical land, modern secular sovereignty, and cultural renewal for the Jews.

Kadima is thus a unique linguistic creature, progressive
and at the same time progress-defying. For many generations,
the Jews stood in the stream of Time with their faces looking
to the past, and their backs to the future. Until modernity
came and shook them up brusquely, turning them in the opposite direction, often as a stark condition for their survival.

Let us assure you that most speakers of Modern Hebrew
do not walk backward through time. We share the Western
imagery of progress. But our own language secretly uses a
different compass. It still follows the ancient Hebraic gaze all
the way to Abraham, shepherding his clan and flocks from Ur
Kasdim to the Promised Land.

Let us now consider another Jewish treatment of time. It is not
linear, not even backward-facing linear. It denies chronology
altogether.

"There is no early or late in the Torah." The first man to
put this principle on record was the Mishnaic Rabbi Eliezer,
son of Rabbi Jose of Galilee. The big cannons of Jewish exegesis, Rashi included, followed suit. Repeating this phrase in
variations, they insisted that the essence of the Torah, original

text or sage interpretation, does not belong on any timeline. It is a corpus of pure, perennial truth.

Nahmanides, for his part, objected. The Torah is not timeless, said the thirteenth-century rabbi, born in Catalonia and buried in the Promised Land. We must pay attention to biblical chronology and the sequence of narrative. This pillar of medieval Sepharad, Moshe Ben Nahman by his Hebrew name, still believed, of course, that the Bible says God's own words. It took the early modern giant Baruch Spinoza to say out loud that the biblical texts are fully and fallibly historical. That they contain mistakes and contradictions, and they should be read with a scientific eye, with a philologist's magnifying glass.

Spinoza suffered for his insight. In 1656 he was ostracized by the Amsterdam Portuguese Jewish community. He was only twenty-three years old, perhaps the first modern Jew, evidently the earliest torn intellectual of modern Jewry. To this day, Jerusalem has not named a street after him. But was Spinoza ejected from Jewish memory? Ask the Jewish youngsters who began to read his works in German during the eighteenth century, among them Moses Mendelssohn and Solomon Maimon. By the late nineteenth century Yiddish discussions and Hebrew translations of Spinoza were available to eastern European yeshiva students to read secretly, under the desk, out of the rabbi's sight. Perhaps some of their rabbis actually read him, too. Spinoza's was one of the first fresh voices infiltrating the vast closed world of Ashkenazi Orthodoxy, chiming the notes of a changing world, and encouraging their well-trained eyes to move to new sorts of texts.

But Spinoza was not the first to deny the very historicity of the ancient narrative, relegating it to the realm of abstraction and intellectual construct. "When was Job?" the Jerusalem Talmud asks, and the rabbis argue: was he a contemporary of Abraham? Maybe of Jacob? Does the Job story run parallel to the book of Judges? Perhaps Esther? Each hypothesis is supported by nice and scrupulous textual evidence. Until Rabbi Shimon ben Lakish gets tired of the whole game. "Job did not happen," he says, "and will not happen." The Babylonian Talmud has a famous equivalent. "Job," it says, "never existed and was never created, but was a fable."

Which echoes Naomi Shemer's comment, and our own stance, in the dispute on biblical archaeology: why should it matter to us whether the biblical stories are fact or parable? The Bible's mismatch with scientific findings does not derogate the Bible. Good stories carry their own form of truth, and there's more than one way to build a palace for posterity. Even the Talmud, whose scholars would obviously endorse the Bible's historicity, dared suggest—at least in regard to the evasive Job—that certain truths are not historical but allegorical.

So the lines are not so clear, thank goodness. Nahmanides is in disagreement with Rashi on the importance of biblical chronology, and heralds the iconoclastic Spinoza. Shemer argues against fellow seculars Finkelstein and Silberman. And the authors of the present book, strangers to much that the Talmud asserts, salute its sophisticated sense of parable and symbol.

We now wander away from the stream of time, whichever way it flows, into the beautiful parable of the orchard. In Jewish literature there have been several famous walks into gardens of trees, all remotely chiming that first walk out of the Garden of Eden. The Song of Songs, for example, has the narrator (a symbolic Solomon? a possible Avishag?) stepping "down into the garden of nuts, to look at the riverbed's green plants, to see whether the vine blossomed, the pomegranates budded." But later generations were far removed from this sort of erotic agriculture. In postbiblical interpretations, of course, the whole Song of Songs is seen as a pious exchange between the People of Israel and their beloved creator.

The Talmudic version of walking into the woods is, unsurprisingly, allegorical. The orchard is the Torah, down to its deepest, labyrinthine, dangerous secrets.

> The Rabbis said: four went in the orchard. And these are: Ben Azzai and Ben Zoma, Acher and Rabbi Akiva. . . . Ben Azzai peeked in and died. . . . Ben Zoma peeked in and got hurt. . . . Acher cut the saplings, Rabbi Akiva came out in peace.

Remember *Acher*? He was Rabbi Elisha ben Abuya before he became "Other," and this story is seen as explaining his breakdown of faith, "cutting the saplings," taking his unrivaled intellect away from the Mishnaic schoolroom, to apostasy, to the Romans, to the alien wisdoms of the gentiles. He was the ultimate traitor, but the Talmud still keeps him on record. Unnamed and unforgotten.

One viable interpretation of the orchard parable is that the innermost depths of Jewish learning are not for everyone. There are grades of intellect and faith requisite to delve deep, deeper, and deepest. In ascending order, death, lunacy, and the loss of faith await those unable to deal with the inner core of wisdom. Only Akiva made it home safely.

Accordingly there are quadruple gateways to the Torah, depending on your standing as a reader. Nahmanides tidied up the four levels of interpretation. His types of exegesis correlate to those discerned by Christian medieval theologians: literal, anagogical, allegorical, and mystical. Subsequent Jewish scholars such as Moses de Léon referred to the four gateways as *peshat, remez, drash,* and *sod:* plain reading, insinuation, inquiry, and secret. Here is a spectrum rich enough to stretch through all varieties of Jewish reading, from the rationalist to the occult.

The first letters of *peshat, remez, drash,* and *sod,* so taught the great kabbalist Rabbi Isaac Luria, dubbed the Holy Ari, combine to make the Hebrew word *pardes,* orchard. Our ancient circle is thus closed. The garden, already a metaphor, becomes an acronym.

Far removed from the biblical nut grove of earthly desire, for centuries the rabbis lived in plantations made of words. Even the Holy Ari, whose abode was the breathtaking city of Safed high up in the Galilean mountains, had eyes only for words. Words and other glyphs, notably numbers, could lead you into the mystical cycles of eternal sagacity. No other landscape was requisite.

Of course, the Talmudists and their descendants did not think that the entire Bible was a fib. Nor did Shemer. Nor do we, in our modern Israeli world, which is made of physical orchards as well as verbal ones. The Bible surely conveys some historical facts. Alongside such facts and unfettered by them, it knows many things that history alone cannot divulge.

What the rabbis did suggest, and we agree, is that the ancient stories can work independent of on-the-ground verification. Fiction, unlike lies or ideological distortions, will invent plots and mess around with evidence, while telling us things about the universe and humankind that we recognize as genuine and profound. As the novelist among us once wrote, facts at times become the dire enemies of truth.

As we exit the orchard, the core idea of Jewish timelessness comes into focus. A mind-boggling idea. It is neither cyclical nor linear. Nor does it allegorize biblical stories. Rather, it says that everything is happening at once. All minds who ever lived are contemporaries.

Take the story of God, Moses, and Rabbi Akiva's meeting on Mount Sinai. It is a chunk of vintage Talmud, and we are grateful to a contemporary Israeli sage, Haim Be'er, for first bringing it to our attention.

> When Moses ascended on high he found the Holy One, blessed be he, engaged in affixing coronets to the letters. Said Moses, "Lord of the Universe, Who stays Thy hand?" He answered, "There will arise a man, at the end of many generations, Akiva b[en] Joseph by name, who will expound upon each tittle heaps and heaps of laws."

We are on Mount Sinai. The people of Israel are waiting impatiently in the valley below. But God is taking his time with the Tablets, crafting crowns on top of the Hebrew letters, and perhaps even attempting a final sneak proofreading. Why is the Holy One so extra careful? Because a millennium and a half later the Talmudist Akiva will show up and turn the Ten Commandments into a full legal corpus.

God's meticulousness is fascinating. We will get back to it. Suffice it to say, at this point, that we are not aware of any other deities (including those of other monotheistic religions) who get caught by a mortal man in the act of chiseling ornaments onto a text writ in stone, for the future benefit of another mortal man. Gods don't usually do this sort of thing.

Upon hearing the almighty's explanation for this slight delay in the Torah-giving schedule, Moses seems a trifle jealous. An intellectual rivalry is born, of the sort so rife in Jewish learning. Such rivalries can easily skip generations. In this extreme case, one Hebraic giant is eyeing the accomplishments of another Jewish master, fifteen centuries his junior.

> "Lord of the Universe," said Moses, "permit me to see him." [God] replied, "Turn thee round." Moses [found himself in Akiva's Talmudic classroom,] went and sat down behind eight rows.
>
> Not being able to follow their arguments he was ill at ease, but when they came to a certain subject and the disciples said to the master "Whence do you know it?" and the latter replied "It is a law given unto Moses at Sinai" he was comforted.

Why was Moses comforted? Because of the reassurance that his name and credentials will be remembered. The story allows Moses to presage the timeless value granted to him in Jewish history, ever-present in future environments unfathomable to him, in future arguments and texts illegible to him. The story takes Moses the historical person to meet Moses the timeless prophet. That meeting is both out of time and deeply cognizant of time.

> Thereupon he returned to the Holy One, blessed be He, and said, "Lord of the Universe, Thou hast such a man [Akiva] and Thou givest the Torah by me!" He replied, "Be silent, for such is my decree."

Is Moses being noble, in a rabbinical sort of way? Is he fishing for compliments, in a human sort of way? Is someone in second-century Mesopotamia busy telling us something about near-contemporary Rabbi Akiva? But Akiva himself remains passive throughout the tale, and it will end very badly for him. Therein lies a dour lesson for Moses on the limits of human eminence as well as human understanding.

> Then said Moses, "Lord of the Universe, Thou hast shown me his Torah, show me his reward." "Turn thee round," said He; and once again Moses turned round and saw them weighing out his [Akiva's] flesh at the market-stalls. "Lord of the Universe," cried Moses, "such Torah, and such a reward!" He replied, "Be silent, for such is my decree."

This is a marvelous story for several reasons. Moses is so human that we could touch him. God elegantly plays his two hands: first, the fatherly familiarity, patiently answering Moses' questions and showing him things beyond his ken. Second, the lordly inscrutability, meting out a horrible fate for Akiva along with a humbling "shut up and obey" imperative to Moses. Such are the boundaries of divine revelation and human grasp.

God must have been in the same mood when he gave his answer to Job.

> Where wast thou when I laid the foundations of the
>   earth? Declare, if thou hast the understanding.
> Who determined the measures thereof, if thou
>   knowest? Or who stretched the line upon it? . . .
> Hast thou entered into the springs of the sea? Or
>   hast thou walked in the recesses of the deep?

Have the gates of death been revealed unto thee? Or
　　hast thou seen the gates of the shadow of death?
Hast thou surveyed unto the breadths of the earth?
　　Declare, if thou knowest it all.

What we find most amazing in the Moses-to-Akiva story
is the transcendence of time. Future gazing in itself is banal:
almost all cultures engender visionaries, and the Hebrew
prophets are among them. Moreover, this is no time-travel
tale of the science fiction or fantasy ilk, because its whole
point is that *Moses did not really travel in time*.

Rather, this is a drama of clashing intellects. A veritable
Jewish topic. Show me two sages, I'll show you a good competition. In modern times Agnon brought this type of plot to
its apex in his novella *Two Scholars Who Lived in Our Town*.
Deeply aware of the ancient lineage of rabbinical disputes,
Agnon was hinting at another Talmudic adage: "Two scholars
who live in the same town and are not mutually accommodating in matters of *halakha*, one dies and the other leaves town."
All this pertains, of course, only to "controversy for heaven's
sake," not to any old quarrel.

In our story, the timeless Author of the Torah—to which his
authorship of the universe seems almost secondary—pitches
two of his greatest disciples against each other. The plot relies on
the Torah's eternal wholeness. Akiva would not have been able
to establish his rabbinic authority among his contemporaries
had it not been assumed that all the exegetical wisdom, all scholarly insights and legal derivatives, were already tight-packed
into the Two Tablets of the Covenant themselves.

But if Akiva is standing on Moses' shoulders, and Moses
receives the Torah from God, isn't this a normal linear process?

Well, no. Recall God's handcrafted ornaments on the Tabernacle, in preparation for Akiva's reading of the same, many centuries to come. God's attitude to Akiva is not only intimate, but also strangely awed. The Torah letters are crowned for Akiva's pleasure. The very Giving of the Torah is delayed for his sake. The delay is significant, so this momentary time does matter, even if the great sweep of time from Moses to Akiva is wiped out. All this is not your usual timeline. It is a metachronological sphere in which deity, men, and texts cohabit and interact.

We can historicize the sequence, of course, and give you everyone's estimated dates in good schoolbook fashion. The storyteller is Rav Yehuda ben Ezekiel (Babylon, 220–99 CE), citing from his teacher Rav (the Talmudist Abba Arikha, Babylon, 175–247 CE). The story refers to three persons who inhabit the distant past of these Talmudists. Moses may have lived (so scholars surmise) around the fourteenth century BCE. Rabbi Akiva was born around 50 CE. God, naturally, is ageless.

But why date the story at all? The Almighty, Moses and Akiva, Rav Yehuda and Abba Arikha are all dwellers in the timeless tent of Torah. Clock and calendar are mere props. Remember Einstein's tongue-in-cheek suggestion that time only serves our sense of order, "so that everything doesn't happen at once"? Here, in a strange sort of way, everything does happen at once. Eras are thrown around, epochs tossed and rearranged like dice. The text is what really matters. Human minds ceaselessly read it and tirelessly interpret it, forever quoting and disputing each other, astride of space and time.

Still, of course, worldly time does matter. The fact that Akiva belongs to the far future of Moses means that Akiva knows more.

Consider the following story, this time of Midrashic origin. Once again, Moses goes up Mount Sinai only to find God busy studying. Moses does not actually see the Creator, but he hears him uttering the text orally, as Jewish scholars love to do.

Why should God be studying? Well, why not? Isn't He *a yid?* This is what one does. One studies.

His study focuses on a scholarly issue from the distant future of Jewish thought. To be precise, God is studying the Mishnaic debate on the Red Heifer. The problem itself is a bizarre hair-splitting affair, which has become an emblem of Talmudic learning in all its trivial nitpickiness or analytical greatness, depending on your viewpoint. A spotless red heifer was a rare and precious creature, and the Book of Numbers describes how it is ritually slaughtered and burned. Its ashes are requisite for purification rituals, especially that of the grand priest. The Talmudic debate dwells on small physical details that might make the heifer ineligible to serve as purifier. And since we don't like spoilers, we will not tell you which recent novel by Michael Chabon makes clever modern use of this ancient lore.

Back to our story. As Midrash Tanchuma tells us, God not only studied the Heifer debate, but also took sides, just as he did in the case of Akhnai's Oven, which we visited in Chapter 1. We like this Talmudic deity, who wants to be neither the Lord of Hosts nor the Divine Clockmaker, but rather the Great Scholar in Heaven. Lo and behold, once again he supports the opinion of the very same Rabbi Eliezer ben Horkanos of Akhnai's Oven fame. But in this story, no one challenges God's intervention. "My son," he lovingly calls Eliezer.

Poor Moses is jealous again, or at least astounded. "Master of the Universe," he says, "everything on heaven and earth is yours—and you repeat a *halakha* in the name of a flesh-and-blood man?"

So God reminds Moses that in Jewish tradition flesh-and-blood individuals can matter very much. "One righteous man will in future stand up in my world, and will open with the case of the Red Heifer." Then the master of the universe goes back to his study, duly and purposefully continuing the point where he had been rudely interrupted: "Rabbi Eliezer says . . ."

And Moses? This time he does not ask to *see* the lucky sage. Instead, he asks to *sire* him.

"Sovereign of the Worlds, may he [Eliezer] be of my loins!"

We have a happy end. God offhandedly replies, "Be sure he is of your loins."

Think of the beauty of this story: it conjoins sons and disciples, biological lineage and intellectual continuum. Moses behaves here like a character from *Back to the Future,* but his hope that Rabbi Eliezer is his distant descendant is mainly about intellectual procreation. Here is our familiar alignment of parent and teacher, the overlap of child and student.

Once again we run the gamut from the Ten Commandments to the most intricate Talmudic analysis, paralleling a family tree. Note, too, that in both stories—that of Moses and Akiva and that of Moses and Eliezer—God plays both the technical role of time machine, and the dramatic role of preferential father to competing sons. He even studies Eliezer's halakhic rulings. But the real drama is between two men: ancestor and progeny, first teacher and remote disciple, early source and latter-day interpreter. It is a drama of humans seeking to become, somehow, as perennial as the ideas they discuss.

And time does matter. The accumulation of years and

eons in the stories of the Jews is of tremendous importance. If time did not matter, there would be no need for Moses to become the ancestor of Eliezer ben Horkanos.

Jewish civilization spans, by its own count, almost six millennia since the Creation, and some three and a half millennia since Moses. If we stay on solid historical turf and stick to our textline, to the solid sequence of books, we still have at least two and three-quarters thousand years on our hands.

Seldom have histories been so controlled by their own protagonists. Of course, external sources mention the Israelites, but what really counted—in the view of the actual players—was packed in textual capsules passed on from one generation to the next. Mordecai Kaplan believed that Diaspora Judaism survived because no one—certainly not the host civilizations, until modern times—took the trouble to compete with Jews for the hearts and intellects of their youngsters. "Judaism functioned as a civilization," he writes, "insofar as it had a monopoly on the first years of the child's upbringing." There is a strong link, we suggest, between the Jews' tight grasp on their own history and their parental penchant for intellectual torch passing.

The annals of the Jews contradict the facile assertion that history is written by the winning side. Even when they lost, and lost terribly, the Israelites, and then the Jews, took great care to tell the stories themselves. They told their offspring bluntly and honestly all the bad things that had happened: sin and punishment, defeat and exile, catastrophe and flight. It is not a pleasant history, but it is consistently and adamantly self-authored. To many children, it was—and is—a captivating, troubling, and ultimately exhilarating legacy.

But it is not an easy history to tell your children. It has more victims than heroes, and, in the past two millennia, no kings and no castles. The knights in shining armor are the Crusaders who disemboweled us with their sparkling medieval swords. In other people's accounts, from Chaucer's *Canterbury Tales* to the lovely lore of Jacob and Wilhelm Grimm, we are the bad guys. And ugly, too. Even the emblematic beautiful Jewess—Shakespeare's Jessica or Walter Scott's Rebecca—was likely to have a hideous father. Such are the strange genetics of anti-Semitism. And when modern racism stepped in, even the Jewesses ceased to be beautiful.

Before the Haskalah of the late eighteenth and nineteenth centuries, Jewish children were not taught history in the Greek, Roman, or modern Western sense. There were exceptions to this rule, chiefly among educated Sephardim and some Italian Jews, but the bulk of youngsters who did study studied Torah. They were taught Remembering, Learning, and Disputing. There must have been an enchantment, at a very young age, that kept so many of them in a small dark heder, later in the ramshackle synagogue, and the rest of their lives in the constrained, isolated, often miserable Jewish existence.

In her book *Israelis in Berlin*, the historian among us asked what kept the youngsters in tow. In the dead of European winter, with Christmas trees twinkling in the village square, with light and laughter in the *goyish* tavern, with straw-haired maidens making merry and golden epaulets gleaming on the officers' broad shoulders, how could the Jewish boys and girls keep away? How was adolescent rebellion contained, duty-bound discipline internalized, and alienness reembraced over dozens of generations? To be sure, many did leave the fold. Countless people forsook the Jewish faith, thereby abandoning Jewish peoplehood, forcibly or voluntarily, and vanished from the chronicles; but sufficient numbers of Jews opted to keep the torch alight.

What those children were taught was no ordinary history. It was not "Jewish history" as we understand it today. It was a different know-how, conveying the sense of a divine presence coupled with a powerful human agency. It was about the staying power of words. In every schoolroom worth its salt, dark and dismal as it may have been, Moses and Akiva and Eliezer ben Horkanos were in attendance. "Turn thee round," a gifted boy could hear a whisper in his ear, "and you can sit on a Mishnaic bench in the eighth row and listen. And when you are a bit older, you will be able to argue, too."

And so, the biblical heroes and the Talmudic scholars somehow insist on being Our Contemporaries. They are the travel-fellows of the learned, but also make their way to the unlearned, such as Haim the porter and his pious wife Hannah. They were the palpable benchmates of all those little boys, and their few fortunate sisters, in Baghdad, Barcelona, and Bialystok.

Within this logic of timelessness it is not so hard to imagine Moses sitting at the back of Rabbi Akiva's classroom. Or even God himself, adjusting his reading glasses, bent over Eliezer Ben Horkanos's ruling on the Question of the Red Heifer.

Make no mistake: these are not ghost tales. No séance was involved, no reawakening of the dead. This is the ever-living company of conversing scholars. Wisdom is immortal.

And still, always and everywhere, the young Jewish student is urged to say something new. Never mind that the Torah is whole and eternal. Never mind that the most formidable minds in Jewish history are watching you from the symbolic back bench. Every boy at his Bar Mitzvah, every bridegroom under his matrimonial canopy, is expected to say a *chidush*. A novelty. Not merely to repeat ancient wisdom. Not merely to ask questions and obey the learned responses. But actually to bring forth a fresh idea, a crisp interpretation, an unexpected link. Surrounded by gigantic bookshelves, you are still invited to make an original statement.

In case you are curious—yes, we do believe that the present-day Israeli high-tech aptitude somehow springs from those intellectual sources. We are talking habits, not chromosomes. Who cares whether any of our startup inventors biologically emerged from Moses' loins? The love of *chidush* is the only relevant genome. Though, on second thought, when modern technology is concerned, a hyperlink to some of the Ten Commandments would work well, too.

Modern Jews developed other time-hopping relationships with figures from their collective past. From the late nineteenth century to the mid-twentieth, when writers and teachers began to use the reawakened Hebrew, biblical protagonists were literary figures of choice. Just like the Zionist pioneers themselves, these Israelite heroes and heroines romp around land, practice agriculture and warfare, and they are not overly intellectual. The new child of the ancestral homeland was expected to be muscular rather than cerebral. But there was more to this biblical turn than the simplistic rekindling of the campfires of Jewish national belonging. Characters in modern Jewish historical fiction can also be brooding and tormented, highly individualized, and at times vainly attempting to flee their Jewish fates. From Abraham Mapu's nineteenth-century biblical romance *The Love of Zion,* featuring Amnon and Tamar, through A. B. Yehoshua's fine historical novel *A Journey to the End of the Millennium,* resplendent with medieval rabbis and smart Jewesses, to Zeruya Shalev's Bible-and-Talmud-quoting women in and out of love, a great chain of inspiration has evolved.

More recently, ancient and medieval Jewish poetry has been put to music by young Israeli songwriters. The sensual, saucy lyrics of the Sephardi Golden Age are special favorites, and so are some resonant psalms and prayers. If you surf the websites of the Israeli music industry, you will find that Shlomo ibn Gabirol and Yehuda Halevi of eleventh-century Spain, Immanuel the Roman and Daniel Dayan of thirteenth-century Italy, and Shlomo Alkabetz and Israel Najara of sixteenth-century Safed are not merely the names of streets in Tel Aviv. These long-dead poets have followers in jeans and dreadlocks, who perform them in concerts and clubs. And, after so many centuries of transmission in print and synagogue chanting, they now have discographies and video clips.

Somewhere, perhaps tucked away in the corner of a trendy cafe in the Tel Aviv street named after him, lexicographer Eliezer ben Yehuda must be smiling. He was the keenest reviver of the Hebrew language for the modern age. He raised his children, alone in the world, on Hebrew alone. He would have loved to hear the biblical and medieval Hebrew verses, those colorful clever words, so close to the hearts of young twenty-first-century Israelis. And so it goes, from Córdoba to YouTube, courtesy of a crazy Russian-Jewish philologist. A textline.

Celebrating Israel's cultural renaissance risks ignoring several great hurts. We do not wish or need to ignore these hurts. The loss incurred by the Palestinians is gradually finding its words, its lineages of memory. A narrative on Palestinians and Words will yet evolve, not here, not by us. But we are not strangers to the pain. Without pushing facile comparison, we can still pledge familiarity. The piercing feel of a world undone—not just lost; undone—permeates both Palestinian and Jewish calamities.

The first Jewish writers and artists who embraced modernity in its wrenched and twisted fullness were not the kind of people who comfortably enjoy their colorful folkloric heritage. They were torn men and women. Their relation to the ancient lineage was never simple, never cozy, never self-congratulatory. Yes, Heinrich Heine could play with Jewish tales and "Hebrew melodies," but he was deeply troubled by Shakespeare's Shylock, and even more so by Shylock's treacherous daughter Jessica. Heine lovingly refused to attribute Jew-hatred to the English bard himself, but he was distinctly pained by middle-class German anti-Semitism in his own environment.

It was Heine's ambivalent modernity that led him to explore, in a Romanticist vein, his nation's ancient lore. He strove to be as German as he was Jewish, and, increasingly, more German than Jewish. "Striking, indeed, is the deep affinity that prevails between these two ethical nations, Jews and old Germans," he wrote. Not only are they both biblically minded; not only was each of them a formidable foe to the Romans; their affinity goes even deeper. "Fundamentally, the two peoples are alike—so much alike, that one might regard the Palestine of the past as an oriental Germany—just as one might regard the Germany of today as the home of the Holy Word." This attempt seems pathetically doomed in retrospect, and perhaps it felt tragic even to Heine himself.

Jews, Words, Germans: these lines by Heine are not only an early harbinger of the tragedy of German Jews. They are also the matrix of all modern Jews who were still well read in their traditional textlines, but already pining for membership in their modern nations, in European modernity, and in global humanity. Heine embodies the catastrophe, for his books were burned by the Nazi Germans in Bebelplatz, and his *Lorelei,* the Germanic nymph immortalized in his poem of 1824, spat in his own face in 1933.

There came a brief and momentous time both in Jewish annals and in world history, when Jews of traditional upbringing met head on the offer, or temptation, of modern existence. For one or two generations, they lived in both worlds at once. This is a case not of dual membership, but rather of irreplaceable amputation: leaving the old synagogue for the world's gleaming novelties. Trading dusty wisdoms for sweet sin and sour uncertainties. Embarking on ships to new worlds saddled with guilt and longing. Yiddish clung to their necks like a heartbroken mother. An ancient bearded figure recurred in their dreams, hunched in the empty schoolroom. This is where Heine belongs, and Sigmund Freud, and Franz Kafka, and Walter Benjamin, and Else Lasker-Schüler. Also Saul Bellow and Bernard Malamud. Each and every one of them was gravely, irretrievably in trouble with Time. They all experienced, in their several ways, the abrupt collapse of ancient time and the bewildering eeriness of modern time.

Typically, this ripping moment lasts only one generation. European Jews made the transition from shtetl to city, from yeshiva to university, from Genesis to Goethe in one lifetime.

Jews from the Islamic world were traditionally more open to the surrounding societies, but they too were lured or coerced into migration, relinquishing an ancient legacy of material and spiritual wealth. In the twentieth century indeed the whole world seems on the move. But the fissure of apostasy, the rupture of relocation, and the strain of industrial-era individualism are painfully high-pitched in modern Jews. Among Zionist writers and thinkers, not a single man or woman was calm or harmonious or peaceful. They were all restless seekers, some messianic, some caught in fierce argument with the God they have left behind, many trapped in a no-longer-resolvable burden of love, hate, and guilt toward their murdered families, their vanished childhood landscape. You see, unlike the Irish, the Italians, and other Old World emigrants, soon after we left the old place it ceased to exist, literally wiped off the map. There was no green grass of home to return to, or even to long for. Jewish émigrés who thought they were burning the bridges to the shtetl, looked back in horror to see that the shtetl itself had burned down, and Father and Mother in it. Their lot was worse than Lot's wife's, but they did not turn into stone. Forced into facing the future, they moved on.

Could the modern Return to Zion, some purportedly secular Jews fervently wonder, mean that the Messiah had come? Not as a person but as a closure of Jewish history, a rounding of exilic open-endedness, a smoothing of all that is askew and dislocated? Some Israeli Jews understood the Six Day War of 1967 in messianic terms. Did not Maimonides say that the laws of nature will not change upon the arrival of the Anointed one, that we shall live as before and owe religious and legal duties as before? Maimonides quoted the memorable Talmudic phrase, "the only difference between this world and the Messianic times is in the enslavement [of Israel] by [foreign] kingdoms." Political freedom for the Jews might therefore meet the standard of "the end of days." And there were Israelis—modern, political-minded Israelis—who truly thought that Messiah's steps could be heard upon the hills of Judea and Samaria.

For if the End of Time is historical, and defined by Israel's national liberty, why not interpret Zionism as the Messiah's audible, nearing, up-and-coming footstep?

This was, and is, a minority opinion. A whiff of religiosity surely hovered about the earliest Zionist founders, but it was an aching and sin-infested religiosity, not a chip off the old rabbinic-patriarchal bloc. The pioneers of Israel, new Hebrew writers and theorists, were mostly too secular to reinvent sacred eschatology. Too modern to implant end-of-time mysticism into Israel's infant sovereignty. And too ambivalent and tormented to experience the joy of independence without the agony of irretrievable loss. The Holocaust could not work as a Jewish Armageddon, the token presalvation disaster; it was too horrible for that role. As to the new political philosophy, nothing but democracy could work for the infant nation state. David Ben-Gurion, a self-taught democrat, was far too realistic and gritty to covet a messianic mantle. And the newly politicized Jews, vociferous and variegated, would not allow him to become even a petty tyrant, eastern European style, even had he wished it, and he did not.

As they move within history and try to change history and shed blood in history, their own and other people's blood, the Zionists can be seen as marching alongside all other Jews of their particular generation or two, caught between the old

Shabbat candles and the new flaming ideologies. The rebuilding of Hebrew-speaking nationhood in the Land of Israel was a profoundly modernist project, not because the nation was "invented," but because the pain of amputation and the chaos of clashing identities are quintessentially modern. As is the piercing sense of un-wholeness, a fidgety and creative un-wholeness, that shadows and prompts Israelis to this very day.

A great deal of sadness is inherent in modern Zionism's dance with the Jewish past. Reentering history, as some of its pioneers called it, also brought the Jews into the largely unfamiliar combatant side of history's killing fields. Obviously, they were never out of history on its other side, that of a helpless victim. Zionism wanted to end Jewish victimhood through "normalizing" our existence, bringing us into the bosom of the family of nations. In some ways, it did. Triumphantly. But thus far, contrary to the founders' better hopes, most Israeli Jews are still intimate with both combat and victimhood.

Samson, a figure of enormous physical power, is particularly appealing to the Israelis. Across the twentieth century, cutting through the spectrum of political ideology, he has fascinated both the revisionist Zionist leader Ze'ev Jabotinsky and the prominent author and peace activist David Grossman. Each of them dedicated an entire book to Samson. Halfway through the century, in the bloody midst of the 1948 War of Independence, an army officer by the name of Abba Kovner was summoned to name the Givati Brigade's new jeep company. He chose Samson's Foxes, after the three hundred wild animals that the rowdiest of biblical heroes set at the Philistines with their tails on fire. The unit fought the invading

Egyptian army in the southern coastal plateau, Samson's own stomping ground. Could any of its bookish young recruits escape textual recollections of Pharaoh or the Philistines? Both its name and its battlefield heroism became the stuff of legend. An eponymous song of praise was penned by Uri Avnery, later an outspoken advocate for Israeli-Arab peace.

Kovner previously commanded the Jewish resistance in the Vilnius Ghetto, fleeing to join the Jewish partisans in the forests. His mother was murdered in Ponar, his brother killed with the partisans. "We will not go like lambs to the slaughter," he proclaimed to the doomed Jewish youth movements of Vilnius, in 1941. Within three years, all but a handful of his young idealistic listeners would be dead.

For the first time in millennia, at the worst moment in their history of survival, Jews became able to choose not to be lambs. In Warsaw and Vilnius the alternative was death through resistance. In the fields of Judea in 1948, it meant becoming Samson's Foxes.

There is yet another Jewish sense of timelessness, the timelessness of frozen moment.

Here, the flow of time is not playfully cast aside to allow remote generations to meet, inspire, and argue. Instead, a particular segment in history, not necessarily a grand or memorable one, stays put. People become trapped within it like a time warp.

In sixteenth-century Poland, frost descended upon Ashkenazi orthodoxy: clothes, furs, stockings, hats, headscarves, and beards all stopped in their tracks. See them today on the streets of Jerusalem, hot and black under a blazing sun. In an important respect, those ultratraditional Jews live in a timeless realm.

Jerusalem itself, from time immemorial, also exists out of time in the minds of the faithful. *Ir Olam,* they called it, eternal city. Whether it lay in ruins, vanquished by conquerors, or was reclaimed by modern Israel, some of its lovers could think of it only as the City of David, young and unravished, a perpetual Temple looming in its midst. Not the First Temple, just the Temple, for it is a futureless city basking in its eternal noontime. For such lovers of Jerusalem, huddled by the Wailing Wall, love cannot be anything but a constant lamentation.

In a broader sense, the Diaspora itself was a frozen moment. Many of the early Zionists, including Theodor Herzl himself, advocated a Jewish "return to history," seeing the exilic experience as a conscious retreat from the annals of mankind. But this observation was not Zionist by origin. In seventeenth-century Venice, Rabbi Simha (Simone) Luzzatto made a similar and merciless point in his *Discourse on the Jews of Venice,* intended for gentile alongside Jewish readership.

> The Jews . . . do not wish at any time to find new ways to enhance the general situation of their people. Because they believe that any significant change that comes upon them . . . depends on a supreme cause and not on human exertions. The order of expulsion from Castile and its neighboring kingdoms . . . applied to approximately half a million persons . . . including men of outstanding capability and state councilors. . . . But in all this great number not a single man dared offer a firm and vigorous suggestion to save them from that bitter expulsion.

Luzzatto's claim is that Jews are meek and obedient to rulers and kings precisely because they accept their historical fate passively. Note the interplay of messages aimed at Luzzatto's two intended audiences: reproach to the Jews and, by the same token, reassurance to their gentile masters.

Reentering time demands action. Luzzatto's grim observation is mirrored in the rallying cry of the Jewish national movement. Yet by the late nineteenth century other forces alongside Zionism made Jewish individuals and groups shift into the modern mode of life-changing human exertion. Exilic timelessness imploded. Jewish history was de-freezing. Men, women, families, and groups were on the move: to America, to Palestine, to modern culture and literacy, to secular self-seeking, and to a plethora of ideologies.

For a vast number of them, it was too late. "Too late" is a term alien to diasporic thinking. God's hand is not tardy. Awaiting redemption by "supreme cause" does not recognize belatedness. But for that yeshiva boy just turning his gaze from Talmud to Spinoza when German tanks rolled into town, "too late" became the first signifier of his shift from exilic timelessness into historical time. The first and the last.

The final Jewish timelessness is void. There is no flowing river from past to future, no coming together of the generations in a perennial schoolroom, no frozen moment, no temple, no black hats.

When called to testify at the Eichmann trial in 1961, Yechiel De Nur (Feiner) forwent his name and spoke to the world as Ka-Tzetnik 135633. This was the Yiddish nickname of a concentration camp (German: *Konzentrationslager*) inmate, and his personal prisoner's number. Thus he signed his books, too.

> And time there, on Planet Auschwitz, was not like time here. Each moment there revolved around the cogwheels of a different time-sphere. Hell-years last longer than light-years.

On the "planet of ashes," denizens had no names, no spouses, no parents, no children. There is no remembrance, no *kedem*, no learning, no argument, no table. Identity is gone. Jewishness is gone. Ka-Tzetnik, too, was dismembered of his name, and kept it dismembered. His Auschwitz is Eden's reversal: Adam gave names to God's creatures. The Nazis de-named and un-creatured them.

In this timelessness, unlike the other timelessnesses, all threads of Jewish continuity and of human existence snapped. Except for words. Until even the words were no more.

Written in a Pencil in the Sealed Wagon
Dan Pagis

Here, in this transport
I, Eve, with my son Abel
If you see my other son,
Cain son of Adam,
Tell him that I

FOUR

Each Person Has a Name; or, Do Jews Need Judaism?

You find that there are three names by which a person is called,
one which his father and mother call him,
and one which people call him,
and one which he earns for himself.
Best of all is the one he earns for himself

WE JEWS ARE NOTORIOUSLY unable to agree about anything that begins with the words "we Jews." For example, who was it who said, "We Jews are just like everyone else, only more so"? We cannot even agree on that. If you Google it, the first ten links will ascribe it to Heinrich Heine, Sigmund Freud, and Abba Eban. But practically every opinionated Jewish individual has something to say that begins with the first person plural. So do we.

This chapter is about collectivity and individuality, an

abiding human theme, "only more so." It dwells on the abstract term *Judaism,* on the plural noun *Jews,* and on quite a few single-person Jews, some of them very individual indeed. We give vent to strong feelings, both negative and positive. By no coincidence, this chapter opens and closes with twentieth-century Israeli poets.

Yehuda Amichai, already quoted in Chapter 1, knew his way around first persons singular and plural. Here is another sliver from his poem "The Jews":

> The Jews are like photographs displayed in a shop
> window
> All of them together in different heights, living and
> dead,
> Grooms and brides and Bar Mitzvah boys with babies.
> And there are pictures restored from old yellowing
> photographs.
> And sometimes people come and break the window
> And burn the pictures. And then they begin
> To photo anew and develop anew
> And display them again aching and smiling.

Amichai has them all frozen in his frame: the collective of individuals that Jews have always been, in their generations of vulnerability, "all of them together in different heights," forced together by family bonds and festive snapshot, huddled against each other under the brutal blows of window smashers and picture burners. The poem now shifts to a new image:

> The Jews are a primeval forest reserve
> In which the trees stand crowded, and even the dead
> Cannot lie down. They rest, erect, upon the living.

Smashed and charred, our calamities have always forced us back to the Beginning, time and again to "develop anew." From Titus to the Kristallnacht, what chance had a willful individual to escape the collective of memory and fate?

Born Ludwig Pfeuffer in southern Germany, raised in an Orthodox family that escaped the Nazis to Jerusalem, he served in the British army, and then fought in the Israeli War of Independence. He changed his name, lost his religion, wrote universal poetry, and spoke eloquently for peace. But he never withdrew from the collective. The new Hebrew surname he adopted, Amichai, means "my people is alive." The post-Holocaust significance of this ancient Israelite name sends a shudder down the spine. Juxtapose it with the postmodernist or anti-Zionist stance, which tells Amichai and his generation, "Your people, revived language, and ancestral homeland are a mere fabrication," and the shudder will turn into a shout. Amichai, however, did not shout. His Jewish-Israeli identity was conveyed in gentle, lovingly ironic verse. Even in his intimate love poems, Jewish fate forever hovers at the foot of the lovers' bed. "Sometimes we are two, sometimes more than a myriad," he wrote elsewhere. The dual "we" inescapably rests upon the plural "we."

And what about God?

Rich in Judaic learning and multilayered Hebrew, sagely reconciled to his own secularity, Amichai was able to write these resounding lines in "The Jews":

And what about God? God remains
Like the perfume of a beautiful woman who once
    passed
Them by and they did not see her face,

> But her perfume lingers, all manner of perfumes,
> Creator of all manner of perfumes.

The latter phrase comes from the Jewish blessing upon scents, from the Babylonian Talmud, "Blessed is the Creator of all manner of perfumes." Amichai knew his *Halakhah,* so he must have known that one says this blessing when encountering various pleasant odors, but pointedly not the scent of a woman. Only a learned apostate, who is also a devious wordsmith, could leave the Jewish deity behind in this singular way. God as the lingering whiff of an unseen female beauty, of all heretical metaphors! How endlessly more intricate, more subtle, more loving and torn, than Friedrich Nietzsche's blunt and pitiless utterance "God is dead."

And yet, Amichai's secular Israeli Jewishness comes from a lineage inspired by Nietzsche.

Some of the greatest Hebrew writers of the early twentieth century rebelled against Jewish collective identity marked by religion. It was a mutiny against that all-embracing abstract noun, *yahadut* (Judaism). In so rebelling, they felt Jewish to their bones. They did not wish to convert to another faith, or to belong to another nation. Rather, in a plagued modernist way, they strove to tear their existence as individual modern Jews from the bonds of traditional orthodoxy.

"There is no Judaism outside our own selves and our own lives" wrote Yosef Haim Brenner, yeshiva dropout, Russian army deserter, would-be but weak-bodied socialist laborer, halfhearted Zionist, tormented soul, one of our best writers. He was murdered by Arab rioters in Jaffa in 1921. Brenner's verdict was both blunt and subtle: *Ein yahadut,* there is no Judaism, outside of us Jews, *yehudim.* "There are no beliefs we regard as obligatory. . . . We are Jews in our very lives, in our hearts and feelings. We need no rational definitions, no absolute truths and no written obligations."

Brenner's peer Micah Yosef Berdyczewski, born to a rabbinical Hasidic family in Ukraine, preferred to demote Judaism rather than deny it. "Jews have seniority over Judaism," he wrote. "The living person precedes his ancestors' estate." In Hebrew, his call resonates with biblical terminology: *Mishpat ha-bechora la-yehudim al ha-yahadut.* Primogeniture, the right of the firstborn, is given to the Jews over Judaism, to the persons over the faith. But this cry for individuation is deeply collective, too: it packs powerful Ancient Hebrew into pathbreaking Modern Hebrew, the reawakened language of new Jewish nationhood, peopled by staunch and powerful individuals.

This may sounds very modern, a fresh "invention" of national consciousness, grist to the mill of recent dissections of Zionism as forged nationalism. Not so. In fact, Berdyczewski, modernist that he was, consciously conducted a passionate discussion across the Jewish generations. Of course he was influenced by modern European nationalism; but the good Micah Yosef also had older sources of inspiration. Like the authors Brenner, Bialik, and Agnon, and like the theorists Ahad Ha'am and Ze'ev Jabotinsky, Berdyczewski could bank on a millennium of debates on the nature of Jewish nationhood.

Ten centuries before Zionism, the sage Saadia Gaon wrote that "the [Jewish] nation is only a nation by virtue of its Torahs," namely the oral and the written Law. So much for a modern invention, or devious forgery, of Jewish nationhood. At least as early as the tenth century CE, we find not only a *concept* of the

Jewish nation, but indeed hints to a *debate* on its very nature. In the twentieth century Berdyczewski and his peers joined that debate with great panache. The Zionist movement—bearing the unmistakable stamp of the European "Spring of the Nations"—raised its stakes to unprecedented heights.

Berdyczewski did not agree that the nation exists through its Torahs alone. As Menachem Brinker shows, he deliberately targeted Saadia in a brilliant counterview of Jewish nationhood. "We were a people and thought so and so, but we were not a people *because* we thought so and so," he wrote. The emphasis in the quotation is ours, and the point cannot be emphasized too strongly. The Jewish people or nation (*am* or *umah,* used interchangeably in ancient as well as modern Hebrew), in Berdyczewski's opinion, exists alongside its religion but also beyond its religion. People and faith cohabited for a long historical stretch, but they are not mutually collapsible.

Where do we stand in the Saadia-Berdyczewski debate, which hopped from the tenth century to the twentieth, and remains deeply relevant in the twenty-first? Our own take involves paraphrasing them both. Tangential to Saadia, the nation is a nation only by virtue of its *texts.* Rephrasing Berdyczewski, we were not a people because we thought so and so, but we were a people because we *read* so and so. As you can see, our differences from the medieval thinker and from the early Zionist writer leave us all on the same textline. If we are fortunate, interesting counterarguments will soon target our own theory of verbal nationhood.

Can Jews exist beyond, or before, Judaism? What does this mean?

Berdyczewski, a rabbi's son gone bad, bad enough to get an education in Berlin and a doctorate from Berne, wanted the nation, "the Jews," to take precedence over the religion, "Judaism." But his understanding of nationhood was quite specific. He was an avid reader of Nietzsche. Like several other early Zionists—the muscular Max Nordau springs to mind—Berdyczewski dreamed of elevating his reviled people to the heights of vaguely Nordic magnificence. Following the German philosopher, he maintained that Jewish persons often possess heroic qualities. Also that Jewish history is first and foremost a history of great individuals and not the history of credos, concepts, or rituals.

However, Nietzsche is not the only source of this "persons first" approach. Both Brenner and Berdyczewski may have harked back to Hasidic ideas. In the late eighteenth and nineteenth centuries, Hasidic rabbis and storytellers embraced a mystical and inherently egalitarian view of individual Jews, not only great sages but also the poor, despised, and insignificant. All are potential interlocutors of the divine. The loner in the forest, the humble craftsman, the little boy shouting wordlessly in synagogue and opening the gates of heaven, the "hidden righteous man" are all Hasidic exemplars of the early modern fascination with the same theme: a particular person who suddenly and miraculously masters a deep and general truth by virtue of his or her marginal existence.

Some of this fascination may have been remotely inspired by Christianity. (Nietzsche himself railed against Christianity, while arguably adhering to its matrix of heroism; but this goes beyond our present story.) The Hasidic attraction to the mute pauper and the uneducated child is certainly uncharacteristic of the age-old Jewish commitment to learned wordiness. This early modern shift toward the poor and the voiceless was an honest and touching tribute to the social realities of the shtetl, to the numerous barely literate, manually laboring, half-starving members of eastern European rural Jewry. But you can also hear the faint bells of Christian lore: the meek simpleton, the holiness of the untaught. If earlier in this book we asserted that there is no *sancta simplicitas* for the Jews, now we must concede some exceptions in early Hasidic folktales. Still, even the most mystic-leaning *rebbes* never placed miracle making above teaching, and no self-respecting Hasid wanted his child to grow in magical ignorance.

Jewish individualism has other roots, deeper than Nietzsche, older than Christianity. We think its sources differ somewhat from the main lineages of Western individualism, although the two strands are interconnected. In this chapter we will walk some way toward distinguishing "Jews" from "Judaism." We will suggest that our enduring collective of strong-willed, texted individuals has more in it than "Judaism."

There has always been a tension field between the collective name *Israel* and the plural noun *Jews*. An ancient tension arose during the first Return to Zion, when Jews came back from Babylon under the leadership of Nehemiah, leaving a great exilic community behind. A comparable tension, involving the same terms, runs through the second Return of Zion and the emergence of modern Israel.

Search "Jew" or "Jews" (*yehudi, yehudim*) in the *Hebrew Encyclopedia* and you will not find it. Surprisingly, this great modern reference work, edited in Jerusalem in the mid-twentieth century by two Orthodox Jewish scholars, does not consider the term worthy of an entry: "Jews—see under *The People of Israel*," it snaps. This, says the novelist among us, is one of the most significant and important spiritual decisions made by the editors, including the rather unorthodox Orthodox philosopher Yeshayahu Leibowitz. It makes lexical sense, too. The term *The People of Israel* surrounds and contains the term *Jew* and the term *Judaism*, and not vice versa.

In the short entry on *yahadut*, Leibowitz writes that this word appears very little in Mishnah and Talmud, and not at all before them. It can be glimpsed in Hellenistic sources, but it is very rare in Jewish literature, even in rabbinic texts, before modern times.

The novelist among us thinks that the term *yahadut*, alongside its English equivalent *Judaism*, is today the identity code of the Orthodox, their tool for correcting the infidels. We seculars are accused of being farthest removed from *yahadut*, while they are the closest. A quiver of guilt-instilling reproach runs through Israel's seismic fault lines, such as the one between secular Hebrew speaking Tel Aviv and its ultra-Orthodox suburb, the partially Yiddish-speaking Bnei Brak. Another rift, less dramatic but increasingly tangible, separates the "national orthodox" Jews from secular Jews; yet both these groups, unlike hardcore ultra-Orthodoxy, coinhabit the modern and largely Zionist mainstream. Such present-day fissures follow a long lineage of ambiguities about the names Jews have called themselves.

The Orthodox context of *yahadut* today ought to raise a smile. Historical irony lurks therein. The very same term, initially in its German form *Judentum*, was embraced by enlightened nineteenth-century European Jews, *maskilim*, and it was especially welcomed by progressive religious reformers.

Judentum was a convenient noun when the need arose to find an equivalent to the names Christianity and Islam. It sounded scientific and respectable. It was the highbrow mirror image of *Yiddishkeit,* the east European "Jewishness" of the masses, warm and zesty and colorful, on its way to becoming the object of bittersweet nostalgia among survivors and descendants of that world we have lost.

The Prophet Amos was neither *Yiddishkeit* nor *Judentum.* If you told him he was a Jew, *yehudi,* he would readily agree that he hails from the tribe of Judea, from the town of Tekoa. But he was not a member of a "Jewish people." This terminology would be as meaningless to him as to King David.

The people of Israel, in all generations before the nineteenth century, called themselves just this, "the people of Israel," *bnei yisrael* or *am yisrael.* And they called their moral commitments *Torah* and *mitzvot* (precepts), not *yahadut.* But in present-day Israel, the newfangled *yahadut* is used by the Orthodox and the ultra-Orthodox to reproach the seculars, who do not measure up to their ideals of religiosity and compliance.

Among Orthodox Jews today, in Israel and elsewhere, *Judaism* is often considered a rendering of *Yiddishkeit,* suggesting that one cannot divorce religion from nationality, or both of those from traditions and customs, or those from dress, or dress from habits, or habits from blind obedience to the rabbis. Jews are expected to be original and not walk the ways of the gentiles. We are told that laying wreaths on tombs or singing the national anthem or shooting guns in military funerals or flying the flag are gentile customs. Meanwhile, they walk the world in the clothing of Polish nobility of the seventeenth century, sing beautiful Hasidic songs based on typical Ukrainian melodies, and dance ecstatic Ukrainian folk dances. They argue with us seculars, at best, according to Maimonides' logic, drawn from Aristotle, or—alternatively—attack the weakness of our national loyalty on the basis of Hegelian arguments, courtesy of Rabbi Kook. But of us, they demand faithfulness to the original fountainhead.

The novelist among us would like to stress that parts of the world of *Yiddishkeit* are close to his heart as a component of Jewish civilization, *tarbut yisrael*. But by no means are they central or unique components. He has nothing against Judaism that adopts reciprocal channels, borrow-and-loan relationships, with other cultures. This is what every culture is about, excluding shuttered ones such as North Korea. And even the shuttered ones are merely denying the truth of intercourse.

Not ours, and not of our origins, is the Aramaic in the Babylonian Talmud. It belongs to the Arameans. Not ours and not of our origins is Maimonides' Aristotelian logic. Even the mezuzah is not originally ours: at least on the outside it is an ancient Persian relic. *Tarbut yisrael*, ever interacting with other cultures, is a great river of giving and a great river of receiving.

The historian among us is less worried about the use of *yahadut* to denigrate secular Jews, and more fascinated by the observation that before the modern age, Hebrew and Jewish vocabularies had no use for a word denoting religion alone.

Berdyczewski's insight that Jews preceded Judaism is true in a basic linguistic-historical sense. If we take our terminology seriously, we are bound to observe that Jews, *yehudim*, existed well over two thousand years before Judaism, *yahadut*. But even *yehudim* is a late development. In biblical times, the people and the faith were usually called after a man: Israel. This, you may recall, is the name God gave Jacob after his eerie nocturnal struggle with a man at the ford of river Jabbok. The man turned out to be an angel of God, and Jacob's name was changed into Israel, which means Striver with God. "For thou hast striven with God and with men, and hast prevailed."

It is delightful, though by no means unique, that the collective name "Israel" comes from an individual's name. Jacob was the third patriarch, father of the tribes, a man of appetite, timidity, and longing, a striver with God, with men, and with women. A prevailer.

Words are important, and so is their absence. Languages do not come up with superfluities. By contrast, when an idea is deeply meaningful it might require several different words. Thus the Hebrew Bible does not have a word for "religion" as we understand it today. On the other hand, it has quite a few terms for the pivotal concept of "law": *hok, mishpat, torah, mitzvah, musar, din, dat.* The last of these, relatively rare in the Bible, came to denote also "religion," but only later, in Talmudic times.

Reading the words in their contexts, many times over, can reward the reader with an increasing sense of familiarity. Despite recent theoretical skepticism, we do believe that an experienced and sensitive nose can sniff out a trace of the original meaning even of very ancient texts. The original meaning! "What the author had in mind"! One can smile at a simile, mouth a metaphor, or taste a turn of phrase, getting a sense of what their earliest listeners or readers experienced. We probably miss a great part of the tenor and "feel" of ancient usage, and often enough we are bound to misunderstand completely, but at times we can grasp it. The careful reader can follow subtle shifts of meaning, trace transformations of a word's role. Such a reader will pick up enough evidence to know that *dat* meant one thing in the Bible and another thing in Babylonian Talmud.

Biblical vocabulary clearly reveals that ancient Israelites understood their god primarily as a lawgiver, and themselves primarily as a jurisprudential community. John Bunyan had a fine phrase for it: "the twelve tribes under the law." Only later came the nonlegalist sense of faith, as in Bunyan's pursuant phrase, "the children of God under the gospel." This fits Christianity better. For the early Israelites, God was the great legislator in heaven.

To get a feel of that Israelite legal culture, please meet the five daughters of Zelophehad, named Mahlah, Noah, Hoglah, Milcah, and Tirzah.

These assertive young ladies could belong to our Chapter 2. But since when do strong women agree to be relegated to one chapter? Gone are the days when history books allotted a lipservice section, usually toward the end, to the female half of society. The five women we shall now discuss are not even mentioned in Chapter 2, which has enough strong women already. We need the Zelophehad girls in the present context, so here they come.

Mahlah, Noah, Hoglah, Milcah, and Tirzah lost their father and had no brothers. The Israelites were almost at the end of their forty-year journey from Egypt, and soon enough each tribe, each clan, and each family would be settling on their promised parcels of land. It is probable that biblical law until that point allowed only the sons to inherit. As a later discussion suggests, the justification for all-male inheritance was pragmatic: if a daughter married outside the tribe, the land would be lost to the tribe forever. But these five women felt an entitlement to their father's future estate. They knew justice was on their side. Mind you, they did not pray to heaven or kvetch to their friends (*kvetch* is Yiddish for "complain," only ten times more sulky). They did what you do when you live "under the law": they appealed to the judicature. Quite a judicature it was: "And they stood before Moses, and before Eleazar the priest, and before the princes and all the congregation, at the door of the tent of meeting."

It was this kind of assembly, appearing in Sinai stories and to a lesser extent in the books of Joshua and Judges, that suggested to early modern European readers that the early Israelite polity was a genuine republic, until the people opted for a king, as the first book of Samuel relates. John Milton and his republican peers in England and even earlier in the Netherlands, in the heyday of seventeenth-century parliamentary awakening, thought that the Republic of the Hebrews should never have been relinquished in favor of a monarchy.

Admittedly, we know very little of the Israelite political institutions. The Bible does not tell us how, if at all, the division of powers between leader and priest, tribal princes and elders, and "all the congregation," really worked. But one thing is evident: this was a society deeply and collectively committed to the rule of law, perhaps the first such society in history. The seventeenth-century English jurist John Selden did not waste his fine scholarly energies when he dedicated much of his life's work to the Mosaic legal system, which he deemed the closest mankind ever got to the quintessential natural law.

But we must return to the five daughters. They entrust their case to Moses and the assembly, granting that their father died "in his own sin," but not in the sort of unforgivable sin that would justify dispossession of his family. "Why should the name of our father be done away from among his family, because he had no son? Give unto us a possession among the brethren of our father."

So Moses took the obvious juridical step: he "brought their cause before the Lord."

Note that Moses neither prayed nor pleaded. He did not await a mystical signal, or flash one of his famous miracles to test out the claim. He simply took this legal case a notch up, to the highest instance. The final verdict was prompt:

"And the Lord spoke unto Moses, saying: 'The daughters of Zelophehad speak right: thou shalt surely give them a possession of an inheritance among their father's brethren; and thou shalt cause the inheritance of their father to pass unto them. And thou shalt speak unto the children of Israel, saying: If a man die, and have no son, then ye shall cause his inheritance to pass unto his daughter. And if he have no daughter, then ye shall give his inheritance unto his brethren.'"

This gem of a story, in its economical way, says something about early Hebrew jurisprudence and social attitudes. Women were not equal, but their reasoning might carry the day, and their entitlement at certain junctures preceded that of male relatives.

The tale continues. When the Promised Land really loomed on the horizon, the girls' fellow tribesmen of Manasseh revisited the case with Moses and the tribal leaders. So just to lay the real-estate issue to rest, God delivered the following injunction "to the daughters of Zelophehad, saying: 'Let them be married to whom they think best; only into the family of the tribe of their father shall they be married. So shall no inheritance of the children of Israel remove from tribe to tribe; for the children of Israel shall cleave every one to the inheritance of the tribe of his fathers.'" Conveniently enough, the young women then married their cousins.

Please do not overlook the offhand "let them be married to whom they think best." We like the way it is uttered en passant, as if women freely chose their husbands as a matter of course. In current ultra-Orthodox Jewish communities it does not work quite this way. And if the in-tribe marriage limitation seems a bit unfair, you will be happy to learn that after the settlement of the Land of Israel, this divine precept was overturned, and women were able to marry outside the tribe, too.

The Torah of Moses came into being as a code of law, centuries before the Hebrew word *dat* was allotted to signify "religion," and millennia before *Judaism* and *yahadut* were coined. The story of Zelophehad's daughters is an account of constitutional amendment and juridical precedent. It is also a chapter in the history of a people assuming sovereignty. Of course, the whole yarn is quite possibly allegorical: five young girls, yet unmarried, reach out like the fingers of a sensitive hand to fine-tune the Hebrew legal system. But it is adamantly not a pious morality tale. The main thrust is that the supreme legislator and adjudicator—divine or human, as you will— took heed and amended the law. Or, at the very least, as the strict Talmudists would have it, he clarified a preexisting law that had been misunderstood. Moreover, if indeed the same law of female inheritance was later changed again, allowing heiresses to marry even out of the tribe, then we have a fine rolling case of constitutional review and revision.

We do not know whether the five Zelophehad daughters ever existed. We like them and hope they did. But the ideas conveyed by these characters most certainly existed, and still do. It is a legacy of "twelve tribes under the law," a loose but intimate federation, harboring inner divisions and clashing interests, diverse mentalities and crisscrossing tribal loyalties, ever negotiating its conflicts and aspirations by juridical means, by argument and reasoning. Even when violence prevails, when the worse traits of human nature take the lead, this community keeps steering back to legality and to negotiation: so many of its stories document the overlap of personal and constitutional dramas.

In short, ancient Israel was a full-fledged political and legal civilization, not a mere flock of coreligionists. Like the five daughters, we too are claiming this legacy as our rightful bequest. Fortunately, the biblical thirst for law-based justice is now shared by most of the modern world.

When do the Hebrews, or the Children of Israel, become *yehudim,* Jews?

The term appears in Kings 2 and in Jeremiah, where it specifically refers to members of the tribe of Yehuda. Jeremiah mentions one gentleman who went by the interesting name Yehudi ben Netanyahu. But then, far down the stream, at the very end of the biblical timeline (though not necessarily the last book to be compiled or canonized), a shift of terminology occurred. The Book of Esther uses *Jews.* The people, now in exile and dispersed throughout the Persian empire, are no longer Israelites in the geographical sense. Their name had changed.

Sometime between the destruction of the First Temple and the construction of the Second Temple, Israelites became

Jews. The biblical narrative traces most Babylonian captives to the tribe of Yehuda, which reportedly incorporated members of a few other tribes—the Binyaminites, the Simonites, and a good sprinkling of Levites. On the rivers of Babylon, the sobriquet *yehudi* was transformed from tribal to national. A nation named after one individual father, Jacob/Israel, renamed itself after his son Yehuda, reputed ancestor of most of those who survived and returned to the biblical homeland. Yehuda, Tamar's father-in-law who unknowingly sired her twins. The stories were alive and well, now etched on papyrus and carved in stone.

The legendary ten tribes of the Kingdom of Israel, already deemed lost, melted into obscurity. The Judean exiles, carrying a formidable history in their luggage, salvaged and reworked their collective identity. Many of them joined a series of homecoming waves, including those led by Ezra and by Nehemiah, adding up to the emblematic Return to Zion in the sixth and fifth centuries BCE. Others may have stayed on the land, never going into exile in the first place, but they were left out of the story. Back in the ancestral land, the repatriating Jews proved highly energetic, nationally conscious, and blessed with a resolute leadership— much like their symbolic successors two and a half millennia later, the Zionists who dreamed and accomplished the Second Return. The Babylonian returnees indeed reinvented Israel: a new temple, a new calendar, new laws against intermarriage, an enhanced particularism, a recently canonized bookshelf, and a new lineage of text-based scholarship.

A large Jewish community, evidently prosperous, remained in Babylon and created the major hub of Talmudic scholarship. Israelites belonged to the land of Israel, but Jews, from the very beginning of this collective title, inhabited a wider world. There is something inherently global about the *yehudim* from their earliest inception.

This is nicely brought out by Zechariah, a prophet who probably returned from Babylon with Ezra. One *yehudi* appears in his prophecies, an early occurrence of the new nationwide meaning of the term.

> In those days it shall come to pass, that ten men shall take hold, out of all the languages of the nations, shall even take hold of the skirt of him that is a Jew, saying: We will go with you, for we have heard that God is with you.

We find it poignant that this early *yehudi* is a futuristic Jew, indeed a universal Jew. He will belong and convey significance to many nations, not only to his people and homeland. Zechariah may have had a knack for new and trendy words, but his usage goes deeper than that: it offers a moment of transition, a symbolic stepping-stone from Israelite to Jew. From a Mosaic tribesman on his ancestral land to a bookish, itinerant denizen of the world, whose God was taken up by many others, but whose status was often far less enviable than Zechariah liked to think.

So let us now take the word *Judaism* head-on. We don't want to dispense with it, heaven forbid, only to stop using it as a cover-all term for everything Jewish. It is too dull to stand in for the histories and identities of the Jews.

The English term *Judaism* stems from Medieval Latin, and the *Oxford English Dictionary* traces its usage to 1251. It was an administrative label, appearing in official and legal documents on fiscal revenue raised by the crown's treasury from the Jews. Robert Fabyan's *The newe cronycles of Englande and of Fraunce* (1516) is one of the earliest texts using *Judaism* in English. But *Judaism*, as well as *Jewry* and their various parallels in other European languages, were used only by Christians. They denoted and, more often than not, denounced Jewish persons or ideas. John Milton wrote contemptuously of "dead Judaisms." Christians suspected of Jewish leanings were accused of "Judaizing."

The Jews themselves, expelled from England during the time when the term *Judaism* took root, had no use for it. Here is a comparative snippet of lexical preferences: the King James Bible chose *Judaism* as the English translation of a term from the second Book of Maccabees, which denotes the Israelites in the original Greek; but a nineteenth-century Hebrew translation of the same verse simply uses *adat yisrael,* the community of Israel.

Other nations called them Jews or Hebrews. The Jews themselves, when donning their learned mantle, stuck with the name *Israel,* which could serve as a plural noun. In eastern Europe the aforementioned *Yiddishkeit* emerged, down-to-earth and intimate. Today it is as nostalgic as old slippers. It smells of Sabbath cooking, yellowing books, silver-bearded rabbis, and sharp-tongued aunts. Since words have flavors, we can tell you that the flavor of *Yiddishkeit* is the opposite of the flavor of Judaism, even if the dictionary definitions of these two terms overlap. As lovers of words know well, dictionaries do not tell it all.

Judeo-Spanish, spoken by Sephardi Jews after their expulsion from the Iberian Peninsula in 1492, stemmed from Castilian peppered with Hebrew and other Mediterranean languages. To denote Jews, it mostly used the singular nouns *djudio* and *djudia,* and the plural noun *los ebreos.* But the more abstract term *judezmo,* which is currently sometimes translated into "Judaism," was in fact a moniker of their language itself, one of the many synonyms of Judeo-Spanish.

As we have already argued, a language does not invent unnecessary words. For many years the Jews, their texts, and their tongues had no use for an abstract term, an "ism," to denote their collective identity.

By the nineteenth century, the term *Judaism* became respectable even in English. Jews now adopted it with relish, mainly thanks to the Germans. Like the academic *Judentum,* it now denoted the whole mélange—Jewish people, religion, cultures, folklore, rites, and customs. In the German universities a new "Science of Judaism" arose, *Wissenschaft des Judentums.* Jewish scholars were now able to join their mainly Protestant peers in pursuing this new discipline. It translated easily into *yahadut,* which is a modern Hebrew word, nonexistent in biblical or Talmudic or medieval Hebrew.

To put it bluntly. *yahadut,* the term that Brenner and Berdyczewski disliked, the concept that weighed on them in its collective mystical embrace, was conceived in the dry scientific bosom of a Berlin lecture hall.

Of course, neither of the present authors proposes to uncoin the term *Judaism.* We know that it is indispensable today, both lexically and emotionally, to Jews and non-Jews, scholars and laypersons. But our own self-understanding as Jews, growing up in modern secular Israeli culture, had little recourse to *yahadut.* The term leaves us cold, even when it is not thrown in our face by an orthodoxy claiming superiority. The stories we are telling here are not about "Judaism" but about

Israelites and Jews, a march of individuals deeply interconnected by texts, striving with God and with one another, kaleidoscopic. Jews and their words are so much more than Judaism.

Which brings us to the languages of the Jews. Hebrew, Yiddish, Judeo-Spanish (or Ladino), and Judeo-Arabic are exclusive to the nation, and all of them are written in Hebrew characters. Great Jewish texts were conceived in Aramaic, Hellenistic Greek, Arabic, Italian, German, English, French, Russian, and several other tongues. Today, some of these are obsolete, and others no longer host significant Jewish creativity. (In the case of German, this phrasing is a chilling understatement.) In our age of linguistic consolidation and fast translation, almost all new Jewish literatures primarily or eventually appear either in English or in Modern Hebrew. So our global conversation, in which non-Jews take part alongside Jews, is now conveniently channeled through two *linguae francae*. There is a tragic dimension to this convergence: so many beautiful worlds and words lost, Yiddish and Ladino almost gone. Perhaps we are wrong here: a small but significant revival of Yiddish is becoming visible among young people in Israel and elsewhere, and the near-dead *mamme-loshn* is cautiously thriving in campuses and in the arts, well beyond its steadfast ultra-Orthodox bastions.

Still, the two major surviving languages of the Jews are Hebrew and English. Both are very much alive in this role. There is still something of a chasm between them, but many bridges are being built; the present book, written in English by two native Hebrew speakers, is one such bridging attempt.

Think of this process as a reverse Tower of Babel. Jews around the world have not been so mutually intelligible since the fall of Judea. Nor have their writings ever been more accessible, to Jews as well as non-Jews. The Internet, a Talmudic tool if there ever was one, is becoming the predominant and ever-evolving space for this latter-day Jewish interconnectivity.

"Back in the Fifties," Saul Bellow reminisced, "I visited S. Agnon in Jerusalem and as we sat drinking tea, chatting in Yiddish, he asked whether I had been translated into Hebrew. As yet I had not been. He said with lovable slyness that this was most unfortunate. 'The language of the Diaspora will not last,' he told me. I then sensed that eternity was looming over me and I was aware of my insignificance. I did not however lose all presence of mind and to feed his wit and keep the conversation going, I asked, 'What will become of poets like poor Heinrich Heine?' Agnon answered, 'He has been beautifully translated into Hebrew and his survival is assured.'"

This, of course, is vintage cultural arrogance. Agnon would be the first to admit it, and the last to care. The whole revival project of our language and sovereignty in the twentieth century probably depended on such breathtaking chutzpah, tinged by self-irony. But the basic claim is valid: Jewish culture was never evenhandedly multilingual. Its gist was always Hebrew, and it rests, at least until the twentieth century, on a Hebrew literary lineage. The Talmud's Aramaic, Josephus Flavius's Greek, Maimonides' Arabic, and Moses Mendelssohn's German all drew direct sustenance from the Hebrew sources. Heinrich Heine's sentimental "Hebrew Melodies" paid a romanticist tribute to a dead language. But make no mistake: it was never quite dead. Not for the rabbis, nor for the yeshiva boys, nor for every Jewish man who prayed in the holy tongue three times a day, nor for those gathered around any Sabbath table. Tens of thousands of books were written in Hebrew during its purported demise, before and after the invention of print, sacred and profane books, prayers and rabbinical responsa, letters and travelogues, grammar and poetry, morals and medicine.

In the realm of sanctity, *kodesh,* Hebrew was always the fundamental language of the Jews. But even in the profane worldly existence that is the opposite of *kodesh,* the workaday sphere of *hol,* Hebrew never totally died. Many of its words lived on in Ladino and in Yiddish. It served in some junctures as a common language for traveling Jews, merchants and adventurers, encountering each other across the Sephardi-Ashkenazi divide.

A great miracle of revival took place in golden age Sepharad, the fountainhead of Hebrew poetry written in Spain, Provence, and Italy in the tenth to fifteenth centuries. From the pens of Dunash ben Labrat, Shlomo ibn Gabirol, Yehuda Halevi, Immanuel HaRomi, and their peers came beautiful texts covering both *kodesh* and *hol,* prayer and eros. Their poetry is alive and well in Israel today, but in their own time the great Sephardi writers could not restore the slumbering Hebrew to everyday life. Already then, no child had been raised in it for more than a thousand years.

Unlike Latin, Hebrew did not die a second death in the eighteenth century. At that time, Europe's scholarly lingua franca gave way to the modern vernacular languages. French, English, and later German took over literature, science, and philosophy. Hebrew, still asleep, was only beginning to flutter its eyelids, called up by the writers and journalists of the Jewish Enlightenment, the Haskalah. By the early twentieth century,

Hebrew had outwitted Latin: instead of succumbing to the modern vernaculars, it became one.

Hebrew reemerged as a modern spoken language in the late nineteenth century. The Russian-Jewish dreamer-lexicographer Eliezer Ben-Yehuda was not the only reviver, nor was he the first, but his Jerusalem home, children included, became the project's most famous laboratory. Rabbis and scholars, Diaspora enlighteners, and Zionist pioneers all took part in this man-made miracle. Stunned observers pointed out that no one had made love in the ancestral language for two and a half millennia.

Wait. We are not so sure. Read some of the sensual verses of Yehuda Alharizi, for example, and judge for yourselves. Admittedly, the medieval Hebrew erotic poetry is highly formalized. It follows fixed patterns, some borrowed from Arabic. To be sure, its biblical sources can pass for mere allegory. But did no Jewish man ever utter something in Hebrew about "a lovely hind and a graceful doe," Proverbs 5:19, in the ears of a woman who might have answered him along the lines of "my beloved is like a gazelle or a young hart," Song of Songs 2:9?

A lot of things are said to sound better in Yiddish, possibly also in Judeo-Spanish, but these lines sound best in Hebrew. If you can't peruse the original, please take our word for it.

Sephardi communities read the Song of Songs every Sabbath eve in the synagogues, and often also around the festive family table. Remember the biblical conjoining of "holy days" with "holy reading"? Well, one may add that Sabbath night is the best, in fact rabbinically ordained, time for enjoying the bliss of holy matrimony. The Song of Songs, as you already know, is the perfect text for the sacrosanct occasion. May we rest our case?

The authors of Sepharad's golden age seem very adept in erotic deployment of biblical turns of phrase. Most of those poets were known as rabbis, and signed their names with that title, but it did not prevent them from penning exquisite obscenities. Allegory? No way. It was a brilliant, shameless, sexual, at times homosexual, poetry of carnal love.

Those Sephardi bards are now one millennium old. That their poems, both sacred and profane, are being composed and sung onstage in Jerusalem and in Tel Aviv, running the full gamut from synagogue to television and from opera to nightclub, is for us a secular miracle. No less.

We consider ourselves uniquely fortunate to have been born into Modern Hebrew, respectively one and two generations after it was rebooted into existence. The Wikipedia article on the Hebrew language tells it in one dry sentence on the sidebar: "Extinct as a native language by the 4th century CE, revived in the 1880s." Here is a bible-size story told in biblical simplicity: a major language was suddenly called to life from its dry bones.

As we have seen, it was never dead in the first place, and there were people able to write and even speak in it during its long dormant years. Still, the feat of revival beggars belief.

Many ancient words were ready for use. Others took on fresh meanings, and yet others were handcrafted from the Hebraic roots by Bialik, Ben-Yehuda, and their peers, including our great-uncle Joseph Klausner. The new syntax is not primarily biblical, but takes after Yiddish and other European languages. Pronunciation, rhythm, and meter imperfectly follow ritual Sephardi Hebrew. Some of these elements reflect conscious decisions made by the earliest speakers of Modern Hebrew. It is a unique, man-made hybrid that became a living, biting, and rather unruly language, happily cavorting with foreign tongues, mainly English these days, and toying with all manner of colloquialism and slang. Nevertheless, Israeli children are still able to read the Bible today, with some help. It may not be the same language, but it is by no means a foreign language, either. Most words spring from the page with a familiar ping.

Modern Hebrew is the greatest linguistic startup in modern times. During the twentieth century, the count of Hebrew speakers in the world grew from near-zero to more than ten million. There are now, by conservative estimates, six million to seven million native speakers and well over three million nonnative speakers, including Israeli Arabs and diaspora Jews. Think of it this way: more people speak Hebrew today than Danish. Or Lithuanian. Or—we like this one best—Austrian German. Who would have imagined?

But the revival of Hebrew would have mattered far less had it not produced, from its earliest modern infancy, worthy literature. Also scholarship, essay, drama, and cinema, all of which speak and echo well beyond the Hebrew sphere. Agnon and Bialik and Brenner, alongside a great many others, were able to climb aboard this old-new platform to write and say valuable things about the human condition, not only the Jewish one. Modern Hebrew culture speaks to the wide world. Conversely, from the very start, it translated and quoted, borrowed and adopted texts and words from numerous other languages. Of all the accomplishments of the Zionist movement, Modern Hebrew is the most creative, the most dialogical, the most global—and by far the least controversial.

Hebrew, of course, was always open to exterior influences. It took some of its earliest words from Akkadian, the primordial origin of our *Eden*. Ancient Hebrew imbibed Egyptian and Assyrian words, plenty of Aramaic, and vocabulary from Persian, Greek, and Latin. Later came words from Arabic and Turkish. For many centuries, the hibernating Hebrew had intimate two-way relationships with its sister Jewish languages, Judeo-Spanish and Yiddish. Modern Hebrew uses Sephardi stress and Yiddish-German syntax, and its ever-evolving vocabulary has good sprinklings of Russian, German, Polish, French, and English, as well as Arabic. In return, Hebrew gave the European languages some wonderful words, which tend to be either very high or rather low: from *hallelujah* and *amen* to *ganef* (thief) and *chutzpah*.

There are many scrumptious surprises awaiting students of Hebrew's foreign affairs. Did you know that the word *macabre* derives from the Maccabees? Or that *cider* hails from *shekhar* (strong drink)? Some even suggest that the German term for marriage, *Heirat,* which has no known etymological relatives, derives from the phrase that each Jewish bridegroom utters at the nuptial ceremony, *harei at mekudeshet li* ("you are hereby betrothed to me"). This hypothesis may not be true, but it is too delightful to skip.

By the same token, some of our best and finest Hebrew words, including bread-and-butter Jewish terminology, were generously supplied by an assortment of *goyim*. Those guardians of undiluted "Judaism" should pay heed. Akkadian mothered the Hebrew words for "book" and "learn." *Kosher* is Aramaic. The *piyut,* our liturgical poem, was shamelessly lifted from the Greek *poiétés.* Even *dat* (*law,* and later also *religion*) was imported from Persian. For "a people that shall dwell alone," the list sounds rather interactive.

Last but not least, the self-congratulating title "The People of the Book," especially beloved by Israeli politicians and producers of literary festivals, comes straight from the Qur'an. Our Muslim brethren grant this elevated title, along with a suitable degree of political tolerance, to Bible-based faiths including Jews and Christians. We are not sure how many Jews know where to place the credit for our bookish national moniker.

Now, if any anti-Semite is reading this (kudos for getting so far!) and hoping to glean support for the tired stereotype of those unoriginal plagiarizing Jews, forget it. Your own language, whatever it may be, is a similar hybrid. All our tongues and cultures are constant shoplifters. Good for them. Hebrew is no exception, but it is a particularly delicious example.

We dwell on Hebrew, though surely not as much as it deserves, because we strongly believe that you cannot do "Judaism" without gazing deeply into the eyes of Hebrew language and civilization. This goes for both Hebrews, the ancient and the modern. In eras when most Jews turned their backs on the world, lonely and loathed in their staunch particularism, their ancient language lay dormant, a sleeping beauty. She was already a hybrid, already impure, full of foreign seeds, till she was awoken into a new world of verbal and cultural intercourses.

But from the semi-Aramaic Book of Daniel to the Yiddish of Sholem Aleichem, and from Maimonides' Arabic to Emma Lazarus's English, whenever a Jewish text sees light in any language, it is always partially fed, overtly or covertly, by a Hebrew teat.

This leads us back to the Jews, a plural noun with numerous singularities. One of the most crucial and typical Hebrew legacies is the centrality of the individual person.

We already said, in passing, that the powerful individualism displayed in the Bible and in later Jewish texts is not your mainstream individualism of modern Western theory. A deep and ancient marker of Hebrew culture is the centrality of the single man or woman, created in God's image, but at the same time belonging to several human pluralities. See how Genesis 1:27, at the very cradle, oscillates between the genders and between the pronouns: "And God created man in His own image, in the image of God created He him; male and female created He them." The grammar itself fluctuates in this compact verse between the mutually complementing poles that are man and woman, singular and plural. This, earlier than the Garden of Eden, is Jewish individualism in a nutshell.

The Mishnah comments on Genesis crisply and lucidly:

Therefore man was created singly in the world, to teach you that whoever destroys a single soul [*nefesh*], it counts as if he destroyed a full world; and whoever saves one soul, it counts as if he saved a full world.

The Babylonian Talmud repeats this phrase with a small and vital change: "a single soul of Israel," it says. Today, some people quote the universal version and others quote the Israel-centered version, at times in edgy political contexts. So let us spell it out very clearly: we are dumping the Talmudic addendum. We are relegating it to the basement, to gather dust among other unwanted heirlooms. The Mishnaic phrase, by contrast, is part of our living room furniture. Each and every soul is a full world, be it of Israel or not. This is our chosen Jewish legacy.

Maimonides, by the way, is on our side. In his *Mishneh Torah,* composed about halfway between the Mishnah and us (give or take a couple of centuries) he embraced the Mishnaic version too, and kept Israel out of it. Well done, Maimonides.

Now this precious idea, that every single soul is a full world, can carry two dovetailing meanings. The first is that each person's life is of tremendous importance. Indeed, since man and woman are created in God's image, each life is holy. Unlike certain Christian and Muslim concepts of the term *soul,* the Hebrew word *nefesh* is almost exclusively linked to life on earth, and not to an eternal afterlife, "for the blood is the *nefesh.*" This can explain to you, en passant, some of the rationale for kosher regulations of ritual slaughter. In our context the equation is this: *nefesh,* the soul in its Hebrew appearance, means full-blooded bodily existence.

"Watching out for the soul" is *pikuach nefesh,* saving other people's lives. Almost all divine precepts can be suspended when life and death are involved. This legal tool is a fundamental law; it can push aside almost any other piece of legislation. Even the Sabbath, says Rabbi Jose. Again, the Babylonian Talmud raises the "Israel-only" banner, implying that one needn't break Sabbath laws to save a gentile's life. We are happy to observe that many rabbis in Israel today, following Rabbi Kook, consider gentile life worthy of saving even on the Sabbath, just like Jewish life. Some think otherwise, and we deem their opinion obnoxious.

The Talmudic sages were not lovers of martyrdom; only three Mosaic laws are worth dying for. They are tagged *yehareg u-val ya'avor,* be killed and do not break: idolatry, illicit sexual intercourse, and bloodshed. Give up your own life, or the lives of others, rather than trespass on these crucial prohibitions. The present authors join many modern Jews—perhaps by definition *all* modern Jews—in relegating the first of these capital prohibitions to the dusty basement. The second requires redefining. The third, the willingness to pay with your (or other people's) lives to avoid the spilling of blood, is open to many interpretations. Among them is the sole underpinning for just war in our age. It is the kind of Talmudic precept that requires caution, dilution, and conjoining with other moral philosophies, not all Jewish. Like many chunks of ancient wisdom, it is too unruly to be permitted to stand on its own.

But the beauty of *pikuach nefesh* is the rule itself, not its exceptions. Apart from the deadly trio we have just listed, every other formidable God-given Hebrew law becomes flexible when human life is at stake. One might call it, in reverse, *Ya'avor u-val yehareg,* break the law and do not die. This is where Jewish this-worldliness stands tall and proud, unwilling to worship martyrdom (although we do have a few well-remembered martyrs), ignoring the promise of a saintly afterlife, and clinging to flesh-and-blood, to the *nefesh.* This is what kept so many *Marranos,* the forcibly converted Jews in Christian Portugal and Spain, behind shuttered windows around their secret tiny flames of Jewish identity. Very few things are worth dying for, and even fewer are worth sacrificing one's children for. When in doubt, opt for life. Deuteronomy has the locus classicus, "I have set before you life and death, the blessing and the curse; therefore choose life, that you may live, you and your seed." And Ecclesiastes, deeply conversant with death, has the Bible's most beautiful little accolade to life: "For the light is sweet, and pleasant it is for the eyes to behold the sun."

And since all men and women were created in God's image, the sun is sweet to all eyes, all lives are sacred, and Sabbath rules must be broken to save every human being.

The second meaning of "whoever saves one soul, it counts as if he saved a full world" is even more fascinating than the first. The same Mishnah chapter spells it out, again with crystal clarity. A mortal man, it says,

> mints many coins in one mold, and they are all alike; but the King of Kings . . . stamped each person with the seal of Adam, and not one of them resembles the other. Therefore each and every one should say, "For my sake the world was created."

The main intent of this passage, in line with the first meaning, is to urge the utter necessity of personal responsibility over the lives of others. Every human being is a unique version of original Man, individually stamped in the image of God. Only the wicked look on at other people's woes and say, "What does this trouble have to do with us?" The rest of us understand, in the words of the Bible-minded English poet John Donne, that no man is an island.

But note the Mishnaic reflection on the matter of human diversity. This is a bonus insight, extending beyond the asserted importance of every soul. In principle, one could have argued for the sanctity of each human life even if we were all essentially uniform, all resembling Adam like peas in a pod or coins in a mint. So the Mishnah has something further to tell us: every soul is "a full world," and every such world is different from all others.

This is not Western individualism but Jewish individuation. The single person is not weightier than the group, nor is the "I" more important than the "you" or the "we." Instead, every one of us must be infinitely important to the others and to the collective, because we are each a unique variant of God's image. Or, if you are secular and claim this legacy, we are each a singular chunk of humanity. Unrepeatable, irreplaceable, and part of a whole.

No wonder that the ancient Hebrew books—Bible, Mishnah, and Talmud—are brimming with the idiosyncratic names, voices, and words of so many individuals.

They all have names. Ever since God called Adam Adam, and Adam gave names to all the animals and to Eve, the Bible seems to love calling people by their names. You can easily imagine hundreds of individuals scrambling up from obscurity, squirming through the mists of time, elbowing one another as they strive to be mentioned, to be jotted down, to be remembered.

Elbow-to-elbow they stand there for all eternity. Meet Elizur the son of Shedeur, Selumiel the son of Zurishaddai, Nahshon the son of Amminadab, Nathaniel the son of Zuar, Eliab the son of Helon, Elishama the son of Ammihud, Gamaliel the son of Pedhazur, Abidan the son of Gideoni, Ahiezer the son of Ammishaddai, not to forget Pagiel the son of Ochran, Eliasaph the son of Deuel, and last but not least Ahira the son of Enan, all of whom somehow managed to squeeze into the book of Numbers, chapter 1.

We don't mean to be rude. All these men were important.

"These were the elect of the congregation, the princes of the tribes of their fathers; they were the heads of the thousands of Israel. And Moses and Aaron took these men that are pointed out by name." Naming matters. Anonymity was never a big thing in Jewish tradition. Not only princes or prophets but also the "thousands of Israel" are forever pining to be seen and heard. This Israelite and Jewish urge to name and be named is about the importance and self-importance of individuals. Also about vanity, for sure. But also about responsibility. The doer must stand behind his deed, the parents behind their offspring, and the rabbi behind his interpretation.

Want more? Try Genesis 11, where the whole male lineage between Shem and Abraham is duly noted; or the endless dynastic records in the opening chapters of 1 Chronicles; or Numbers 26, again a long list of names . . . wait. This one is interesting.

At first blush it appears to be a census of all combat-worthy men, whom God commands Moses to count before entering the Land of Israel. But halfway down the list a woman appears —an Israelite amazon?—named Serah, the daughter of Asher. Then, if you read on, you will see that the census is not really about men-in-arms, but about the future allotment of property in the ancestral land:

And the Lord spoke unto Moses, saying: "Unto these the land shall be divided for an inheritance according to the number of names. To the more [numerous families] thou shalt give the more inheritance, and to the fewer thou shalt give the less inheritance; to each one according to those that were numbered of it shall its inheritance be given." (Numbers 26:53–54).

Notice the link between naming, entitlement, landed property, and belonging. Note that the new Israelite state, soon to be conquered and settled, is conceived as a veritable republic. By this we mean a polity where numerous citizens, all propertied on a fairly equal basis, none too rich, none too poor, form the backbone of a stable civil society. It is based on the political strength of the many, not the few and not the one.

Republic and *citizen* and *civil* are not Hebrew words. They are Roman. Indeed, Greeks and Romans were the first to create a political theory of the republic, alongside other forms of government. The Hebrew Bible, which contains some very political moments, is not a textbook of political philosophy. But the historian among us and some of her colleagues are convinced that a great deal of political *thinking* is immersed in the biblical legislation, in some of the biblical narratives, and in some of the prophetic and poetic texts. What the Book of Numbers reveals here, a crucial insight easily lost in the long lists of Amminadabs and Ahiezers, is that the early Israelite state was conceived as an agrarian republic of near-equal small landholders, laid out as a confederation of tribes dwelling in their respective geographic parcels. A realm of distributive justice.

Perhaps it was so conceived only in retrospect, only as wishful thinking, but nevertheless it was a noble idea: the "twelve tribes under the law," under their God, and under their meticulous textual records.

And therefore, Josephus Flavius was not wholly wrong when he categorized ancient Israel, for the convenience of his Greco-Roman readers, as a "theocratic republic." Not theocratic as in a mullah regime, but theocratic in the sense that its constitution was ascribed to the great legislator in heaven, who subsequently stepped back, leaving his people to their earthly devices under the Law. Whether God exists, or whether God is Law, is almost beside the point. What fascinates us is that under this God or this Law a society flourished, in real history or in later wishful narrative, which attempted to keep almost all its people propertied, on a fairly equal footing. The Jubilee restored property to original owners who had been unfortunate enough to lose it. The sabbatical year allowed slaves to walk free and debts to be dropped. Everyone was supposed to remain, on the whole, free and fed and respected.

It was not only about property. The old anti-Semitic cliché bonding Jews with money misunderstands the intricacy of Jewish moral economy, which cherishes ownership and at the same time strictly delimits it for the sake of higher ends. In ancient Israel—real or imagined—a plethora of solid small proprietors meant a broad constituency of active political participants. Individuals with voices.

Lower down the social echelon, among the landless, no one was supposed to remain hungry or unclothed, neither the widow not the orphan nor "the stranger among you." Naomi and Ruth belonged to that class when they came to Bethlehem. But the sheaves of wheat they collected on the margins of Boaz's field were not charity, not a favor, not out of the goodness of Boaz's heart.

Ancient Israel, you see, was a culture of law-based justice, not kind-hearted philanthropy. That wheat was no longer Boaz's property. It was the rich man's legal levy, and the poor women's rightful desert.

So who was Serah, daughter of Asher, who got herself into the all-male list of heads of families entitled to landed property in

Israel? The lady is already mentioned in the book of Genesis, and some interpreters thought she lived to the ripe old age of a few thousand years. Midrashic tales granted her all manner of magical knowledge, including "the secret of redemption," thanks to her supposed longevity. But if we take the context seriously, and remember that Serah appears in a population survey geared toward real-estate entitlement, we might reasonably suspect that here was yet another very strong woman, or her descendants, claiming yet another exception to the rules of male inheritance.

Lo and behold, here come the daughters of Zelophehad. They follow Serah in the very next chapter, Numbers 27. This should not surprise us: their story is a logical part of the census story, representing a rare case of an all-female family. As you recall, the Bible duly names them, all five of them, and God accepts their appeal and commands Moses to grant them their share of the land.

We are sure you won't mind if we repeat their resonant names: Mahlah, Noah, Hoglah, Milcah, and Tirzah. Of course, these names sound somewhat legendary. It has been noted that the biblical territory of Manasseh, astride the river Jordan (and covering bits of today's Jordan, the Palestinian Territory, and Israel), has at least three geographical place names that ring very similar to the names Mahlah, Hoglah, and Tirzah. Were these the historical estates of the three daughters? Or perhaps, conversely, the legend of the five sisters grew from these ancient place names?

The daughters of Zelophehad may well have been the stuff of fairytale, alongside the three daughters born to Job after rising from his calamity—Jemima, Keziah, and Keren-happuch. Why should one assume that any of these names belong to historical persons, to flesh-and-blood women? When it comes to Job's daughters, our own gut feeling as readers corresponds to the Talmudic line we quoted in a previous chapter: Job never existed, he was but a fable.

Except for one strange coincidence.

As you may recall, Job gave his daughters "inheritance among their brethren." Juxtaposed with the Zelophehad story, this sentence leaps off of the page. The case of Job's daughters is even more radical, because Jemima and her sisters were not the last of their male lineage. But one gets the feeling that a certain common theme is at work. Perhaps the Book of Job is consciously paraphrasing the case of Zelophehad's daughters from the Book of Numbers. Perhaps the intended audience was expected to recognize the allusion.

Fable or historical reality, we will probably never know. But we do have a conceptual and verbal link running underground, connecting different biblical books and eras and genres. This link, certainly in the case of men, and more rarely but more poignantly in the case of women, is between being named and being important, entitled, self-standing.

Our Bible is thus an enormous Noah's Ark, filled with men and women escaping the deluge of oblivion. The wish to be named is reflected in the legal system—or did the legal system echo the ambience of strong personalities?—in which recognition, dignity, and property worked together. Often enough, as in the case of Zelophehad's daughters, it also helped to be vocal, daring, opinionated, and unafraid of old men with beards.

The Talmud, too, is brimming with individuals, in its lettered and masculine way. Some quotations remained unattributed, but no one opts for anonymity. No one is too modest to be mentioned by name. No one creates without a signature, as medieval Christian artists were often expected to do, for the love of God alone.

If you open the Talmud for the first time, the sheer number of names on each page will strike you. About 120 *Tanaim* (Mishnah sages) and 760 *Amoraim* (Talmud sages) are known by name. Some researchers go far higher, estimating the numbers of Talmudists in both Babylon and Israel at more than 2,000, even 3,400. We are not talking about quality here, just quantity. In fact, we think that a dozen Greek philosophers, playwrights, and historians gave the world a finer written legacy than those thousands of Talmudists. With all due respect to the Book of Numbers, cultural greatness is not measured by numbers.

But there is something spellbinding about that sheer mass of learned rabbis. It is utterly astounding to find so many individuals, huddled in two disparate communities of a small nation on the losing side of military and political history, pursuing intellectual activity for its own blessed sake.

Both the Land of Israel Talmudists and their Babylonian peers lived in relative poverty, under the yoke of foreign rulers. We have already mentioned that many of them worked hard to make ends meet: cobblers, blacksmiths, traders. But at any given time from the second century BCE, numerous Jewish men are known by name thanks to their scholarship. Let us sharpen the point. From late antiquity until early modernity, most of the Jews on historical record are on record *because they studied.*

They no longer had prophets or kings. Their scholarship did not flourish in the palaces and academies of victorious empires. Their culture did not breed heroes and soldiers to defend them, princes to patronize them, or benefactors to buy them books and scientific instruments. Their humble heroism was acted out between lowly schoolroom walls, loathed by the gentiles, vulnerable and unsung. Words were their cathedrals.

When Brenner wrestled with Judaism's impositions, and when Berdyczewski insisted that seniority should be given to Jews over Judaism, they were talking like true early-twentieth-century modernists. Their provocative words marked an "individualistic turn," inspired by new philosophy, mostly German. But they were also toeing the line with some very old Hebrew and Jewish traditions. Brenner and Berdyczewski felt, as we too sometimes feel, that "Judaism" is a convenient and conventional abstraction that risks glossing over the bottomless differentials of the Jews. The understanding that every soul is a full world.

Of course, community is of tremendous importance. The Jewish individual is defined by others, even as he or she disputes and quarrels with them. And also defined by the laws, even if he or she chooses to appeal against them, rebel against them, or flatly ignore them. As long as we still have our common words, we are a community. And community has been a natural mode of Jewish existence from Jacob's bustling tents to today's reawakening kibbutzim. Even Tel Aviv, crowded with highly individualistic self-seekers, is more intimate and familiar and public-voiced than any other big city we know.

No man is an island, wrote the great Donne. The novelist among us adds: true, no man is an island, but we are all peninsulas. Partially on our own, surrounded by the dark waters, and partially linked to a continent, to other peninsulas, to the plural noun.

We end with a singular modern Hebrew poet who signed her works only by her first name, Zelda. Back in Jerusalem of the 1940s, she was the beloved second-grade teacher of the novelist among us. And she was the niece of the great Rabbi of Lubavitch. None of his Hasidim would dare read her now; we are hoping that some of their wives secretly do.

One of Zelda's best-known poems, "Each Man Has a Name," is her take on the quotation from Midrash Tanhuma used as a epigraph for this chapter. It was put to music, and Israelis love singing it on the sad remembrance days commemorating the Holocaust and the Israeli-Arab wars. Here it is, in part.

> Each Man has a name
> Given to him by God
> And given to him by his father and mother.
> Each man has a name
> Given to him by his height and the way he smiles
> And given to him by the cloth. . . .
> Each man has a name
> Given to him by his sins
> And given to him by his longings. . . .
> Each man has a name
> Given to him by the sea
> And given to him by his death.

But the Israelis are getting it wrong. Zelda's poem is not only, and not mainly, about death. It is about life. It touches on that old Jewish individuality-in-belonging that stamps each person with the seal of Adam, without any one resembling the other, and without anyone being totally alone.

This truth is deeper than Jewish. It is universal. We are all given our identities by other persons and by other things. We are named by everything we ever knew and by everything we ever did.

Her full name, by the way, was Zelda Schneersohn-Mishkovsky.

Epilogue

But thou, O Daniel, shut up the words, and seal the book, until the time of the end. Many shall run to and fro, and knowledge shall be increased.—Daniel 12:4

Hot er gesogt!
Yiddish saying. Literal translation: So he said! So what!? Why should *you* care?

IN THIS LITTLE BOOK we try to say something of our own about the longitudes of Jewish history. Perhaps you discerned some residues of a dialogue between the two authors, even arguments at times: a bit of an intergenerational conflict, differing gender perspectives, or the subtle skirmishes of fiction and nonfiction. In other words, we hope we fit into the plot, albeit as minor characters.

There is no possible way of acknowledging all sources of

wisdom that inspired this book. Some are mentioned in the text, including a few contemporary scholars, and some more are listed in our acknowledgments and list of sources. Efforts were made to give credit where credit is due, but how can we thank all the architects and builders of the city of words in which we reside?

"Your children are not your children," wrote Khalil Gibran, a Lebanese-American poet. "They are the sons and daughters of Life's longing for itself." Being stereotypically Jewish parents, we cannot concede possession of our offspring quite so easily. But we could paraphrase Gibran thus: Your ideas are not your ideas. They are the progeny of the bookshelf on your wall and of the language that you inhabit.

As nonspecialists in Jewish history, we reached out to it from our respective fields of European intellectual history, literature, and storytelling. On the road, we may have irked both academic specialists and Orthodox believers. Disputes, though, are welcome. We would be perfectly willing to stand corrected by (or keep arguing with) the former, and to stand apart from (but keep arguing with) the latter. May our controversies keep sizzling. May we all be locking horns to the end of time, running to and fro, and knowledge shall be increased.

In the meantime, as the old Jewish saying goes, please do not take everything to heart. It's not healthy for you. *Hot er gesogt!* It's only words.

But before we shut up the words and seal the book, as the prophet Daniel so aptly put it, we want to say a few more things about the crisscrossing avenues of jest, self-recrimination, and argument.

We know you've heard this one before, but please bear with us.

> So a Jewish grandmother walks on a beach with her
> beloved grandson when a big wave suddenly sweeps
> the boy underwater. "Dear God Almighty," cries
> Grandma, "how can you do this to me? I suffered all
> my life and never lost faith. Shame on you!" Not a
> minute passed by, and another big wave brings the
> child back to her arms safe and sound. "Dear God
> Almighty," she says, "that's very kind of you, I'm sure,
> but where's his hat?"

An oldie, we know, but a true classic. What is this joke really about?

On the face of it, of course, it is about the Jewish grandma, who is essentially a hefty double portion of the Jewish mother. As we have already mentioned, we are not averse to Jewish mother jokes, because many of them secretly serve as wry little hymns to their feisty subject matter. So yes, Granny is blatant, impudent, guilt-instilling, and nitpicking, even when her interlocutor is the Creator of the Universe himself. Nice. But wait, there's more.

Where is God in this story? He might not be there at all. It could be a tale of two waves, a woman, and her grandchild. But assuming the all-knowing deity sent both waves, he seems, excuse us, a bit of a weakling. What was he thinking? An Orthodox apologist would be quick to explain that God may have been testing Grandma. *Azoy*. To us heretics, it seems more likely that Grandma was testing God.

Now look deeper. There is a bold theology therein. We are no longer joking.

Unlike most believers of most religions, our Grandma

does not conflate faith with awe. She treats the Lord of Hosts with a healthy pinch of chutzpah. Scrupulous and stingy, impertinent and impolite, she is nevertheless magnificent in her unsentimental devotion. But devotion to whom, exactly? To grandson or to God?

Careful. You don't truly want to test these two grand-maternal devotions against each other. God himself doesn't really want to know. And since we are personally acquainted with Grandma, we can tell you that after the joke officially ended, it is very likely that he humbly returned the hat.

For as we have tried to convey in this book, while numerous generations of Jews devoutly believed that without God there would be no grandchildren, deep in their hearts they also knew that without grandchildren there would remain no God.

There is a Jewish theology of chutzpah. It resides in the subtle juncture of faith, argumentativeness, and self-targeting humor. It amounts to a uniquely irreverent reverence. Nothing is too holy to deserve the occasional send-off. You can laugh at the rabbi, at Moses, at the angels, and at the Almighty too.

Jews have a long legacy of laughter, often adjacent to our long legacy of tears. There is a solid tradition of bittersweet self-criticism, often to the point of self-deprecation, which has proven a trusty instrument of survival in a hostile world. And since laughter, tears, and self-criticism are almost always verbal, all of them flow smoothly into the Hebraic and Jewish habit of disputing everything and arguing with everyone: one-self, one's friends, one's enemies, and sometimes God.

Our granny on the beach is not considered blasphemous

by anyone we know. The Hebrew Bible set the tone with both Abraham and Job haggling with the Almighty over what they see as poor performance in hands-on divine intervention. Then came the Talmud sages, whom we have met in the exquisite tale of Akhnai's Oven, telling a voice from heaven to buzz off and stop interfering with a scholarly debate.

If God could be treated in this way, no great hero or famous rabbi is exempt. In a joke hailing from Vilnius, a local Jewish wit was asked how come King Solomon's bed was guarded, as the Song of Songs (3:7) tells us, by no fewer than "sixty heroes around it, of the heroes of Israel." Why so many? Well, the answer is in the text, he said. Those were sixty *Jewish* heroes, after all!

Do you consider this self-derisive? We do. Deliciously so. If you can stomach a little more, here is a send-off aimed at Hasidic miracle workers:

> The Old Rabbi and his entourage came to a Jewish tavern, and the innkeeper was brazen enough not to step out to welcome them. In his anger, the Rabbi decreed: "Let this roof beam, under which no righteous man resides, become a slanted serpent!" [Even in his anger, you see, the Old Rabbi remembered his Isaiah 27:1.] Everyone was shocked, and the innkeeper and his wife begged for forgiveness. Overcome with pity, the Old Rabbi took back his curse. "May the roof beam remain a roof beam!" he thundered.
>
> And, what do you know? Lo and behold, the roof beam remained exactly as it had been. People from all over the world still come to see that tavern and witness that miraculous beam.

As you may have noted, biblical expressions have always served as excellent fuel for jokes. Thus, as we saw on the Internet the other day, an Israeli yeshiva student today can fiendishly apply the term "seized by trembling," originally describing the mighty Moabites dreading the Israelite God (Exodus 15:15), to his own cellular phone, as he puts it on buzz mode before the rabbi enters the room.

Nothing is too holy, too feared, or too beloved to be lampooned. As with Grandma, so with God: often, there is a wry little hymn tucked into the joke. But sometimes it is merely, plainly, and delectably wicked.

From Moses and Isaiah to Shmuel Yosef Agnon and Philip Roth, Jews have been quick to verbalize their own deficiencies, individual or collective, with the panache of the skillful self-analyst on the run. "No matter how bad things get, you got to go on living, even if it kills you," said Sholem Aleichem, the doyen of eastern European Jewish humor. He meant what he said: often enough it did kill you.

In modern times, in the Diaspora languages of Judeo-Spanish, Yiddish, and English, Jewish folklore and literature opened their floodgates of hapless hilarity. We must give Judeo-Spanish its due credit as a fountainhead of humor—often ironic or sarcastic —that viably vies with Yiddish. "*Wa llego Mose, wa ya me alegri!*" they would say in the Jewish Hispanic communities of northern Morocco. "Well, Moses finally came, and you can see how happy that makes me!" This sort of bittersweet jest easily bonds with the Yiddish brand. The Sephardi-Ashkenazi line could be rather porous, both ethnically and culturally (witness southern France, Italy, and the Balkans, climbing up to Bessarabia and Ukraine, where some of the present authors' family forebears carry

Sephardi names). And why shouldn't Judeo-Spanish and Yiddish develop corresponding humor? Their intellectual engines—for all good humor has intellectual engines—are similar. So are the collective psychologies. Jewish fate and longing, memory and exile, calamity and verbal armor, and that irreverent reverence which is one of our most persistent Jewish longitudes, they are all there. The checklist works for Sephardis and Ashkenazis alike.

So Moses might come, and we will still be complaining. "I know we are the chosen people," goes another classic Sholem Aleichem remark, "but God, couldn't you choose someone else for a change?" For his part, Woody Allen created a new creed of sorts, the Atheism of the Inept: "How can I believe in God when only last week I got my tongue caught in the roller of an electric typewriter?" And, to add insult to sacrilege: "Not only is there no God, but try getting a plumber on weekends."

Israelis try to follow suit, especially when they manage to avoid the dramatized self-righteousness that is the silent killer of sobering self-humor. "Well," asked the BBC reporter, "you have been praying at the Wailing Wall for peace between Jews and Arabs these last thirty years. How does it feel?"—"Like talking to a brick wall," answered the Jerusalem rabbi.

People who think that God and his prophet are no laughing matter deserve respect; perhaps even envy. A triumphant history has left Allah and Mohammed untouchable in the eyes of the faithful. Three millennia of trouble have left Moses, along with his God, exposed to murderous foes as well as scathing insider jest. "Forty years in the desert," snapped Golda Meir, "and he finally managed to lead us to the one place in the Middle East where there is no oil!" Her ultra-Orthodox coalition partners could not but heartily agree. Yet, tellingly, Jewish identity was not weakened one iota by this irreverent reverence; if anything, it keeps atheists like us in the fold.

Yes, the humor is often rude and coarse. If Jews are rather lax about blasphemy, why should they worry about a bit of indelicacy? But given the choice between vulgar wit and refined fanaticism, we'd opt for vulgar wit any time. Let morbid rectitude and learned chutzpah compete: the latter is likely to win the day, or the millennium. So here's to our license, as old as Genesis, to laugh at Granny and God, King Solomon and the Old Rabbi, along with all our other holy relics, to our heart's content.

And God? If he exists, he must be Jewish. If he is Jewish, he surely understands some Ladino or Yiddish. If he understands some Ladino or Yiddish, he surely knows what to say if some lowly joker from Morocco or Vilnius, Jerusalem or New York pokes fun at him. *Hot er gesogt!* So he said! So what!? Why should *I* care?—God would say with a shrug.

Come to think of it, why joke against the Almighty when you can sue him? Several Hasidic tales have ordinary Jews taking God to rabbinical court, *din torah*, demanding that He owes them some desperately needed reprieve. These plaintiffs mostly win their day in court, too. But since laughter and tears are intimate neighbors in Jewish history, this extraordinary practice follows a horrible path. The great-grandchildren of those Hasidic claimants must have been those Auschwitz prisoners that Elie Wiesel reported to have heard attempting to prosecute the Almighty for treating the Jewish people in such a terrible way. Years later, the memory inspired him to write his play *The Trial of God* (1979), in which Wiesel chose to locate that particular court case in 1649, following a massacre of the Jews in the Ukrainian town of Shamgorod (perhaps the historical Shargorod). In this case, God walks scot-free, declared innocent, defended by a charismatic stranger who turns out to be Satan himself.

But how Jewish is this theme? Didn't Dostoevsky have his Grand Inquisitor interrogate and try a reincarnated Jesus Christ, and find him guilty, as Ivan Karamazov hallucinates? Yes, of course. But Jews do not have Grand Inquisitors, lordly and poised, equally awe-inspiring in their cardinals' robes and monkish cassocks. Only abjectly poor and helpless Jews, paupers and concentration camp inmates, bring their Maker to justice. While Dostoevsky's moment was grand and unique, our theme threads in and out through many centuries. While Dostoevsky's divine trial was grim and somber, ours have been tinged by irony, and sparkled by the humble audacity of marginal and insignificant folk. A people who could rage against their God could also laugh at him, win an argument against him, indict and convict him.

Not that this was common practice. Few Jews could ever rise to the challenge of taking God to a court of law. But every Jew who ever read the scriptures was likely to come across Abraham's resounding reproach: Will the Justice of all the earth not do justice?

And this, too, is one of the best questions in the Bible.

The Jews never had a pope.

The novelist among us likes to say that we couldn't possibly have a pope. Because suppose we did have one, everyone would be slapping him (or her?) on the shoulder, saying that their grandmother knew his grandfather in Plonsk or in Casablanca. Two degrees of separation at most. Familiarity, intimacy, contrariness—this is the stuff our communities are made of. Each rabbi has a counter-rabbi, everyone had a crazy aunt, and even the leading lights are a little laughable. No single spiritual leader can unite the entire flock unquestioningly under him, at a suitably mystic distance. Someone will always dissent and object; the smoke will never be white. So much for a Jewish pontiff.

And so we keep arguing. Abraham with his Maker, Tamar with the tribal elders, prophet with king, Hillel with Shammai, Hasids with "opposers," Orthodox with secular. Israel is "striver with God," and the Jewish deity himself can be surprisingly mild to those who laugh at him or wrestle with him, from Matriarch Sarah to the Grandma with the hat.

What makes him so lenient as to suffer such brazenness? Why does he haggle with Abraham over the number of righteous men to keep Sodom alive, and lovingly accept Job's dispute against the very core of divine justice? How can he say, laughing with joy, "My sons have defeated me, my sons have defeated me"?

We do not know. We do not believe in him, anyway. But we think it has something to do with the Jewish way with words, and also with parenting.

In 1982 the novelist among us visited the West Bank settlement of Ofra and conducted a heated debate with the settlers. We would like to quote what he said there, because every word is still relevant to us, and fitting for the closure of this book.

Judaism is a civilization. And one of the few civilizations that have left their mark on all of mankind. Religion is a central element in the Jewish civilization, perhaps even its origin, but that civilization cannot be presented as nothing more than religion. From the religious source of that civilization grew spiritual manifestations that enhanced the religious experience, changed it, and even reacted against it: languages, customs, lifestyles, characteristic sensitivities (or perhaps it should be said sensitivities that used to be characteristic), and literature and art and ideas and opinions. All of this is Judaism. The rebellion and apostasy in our history, especially in recent generations, they are Judaism too. It is a broad and abundant inheritance.

And I see myself as one of the legitimate heirs: not as a stepson, or as a disloyal and defiant son, or a bastard, but as a lawful heir. And what follows from my status as an heir will certainly cause you people great unease. For it follows that I am free to decide what I will choose from this great inheritance, what I will place in my living room and what I will relegate to the attic. Certainly our children have the right to move the floor plan around and furnish their lives as they see fit. And I also have the right to "import" and combine with my inheritance what I see fit—without imposing my taste or my preferences on another heir, on you for one. That is the pluralism I praised earlier. It is my right to decide what suits me and what doesn't. What is important and what is negligible and what to put into storage. Neither you nor the ultra-Orthodox nor Professor Leibowitz can tell me in whatever terms that it's a package deal and I should take it or leave it. It is my right to separate the wheat from the chaff.

And from this follows another fateful spiritual decision. Can any civilization survive as a museum, or does it only live when it wears the garb of dramatic improvisation?

A museum curator relates ritualistically to his [or her] ancestral heritage. On tiptoe, in awe, he arranges and rearranges the artifacts, polishes the glass cases, cautiously interprets the significance of the items in the collections, guides the astonished visitors, convinces the public, and seeks, in due time, to pass on the keys of the museum to his sons after him. The museum curator will proclaim Holy Holy Holy. He will also proclaim "I am too humble to determine what is important here and what is less important. It is my lot only to see that the light of the inheritance shall shine in as many eyes as possible, and that nothing is damaged or lost."

But I believe there can be no vital existence for a museum civilization. Eventually, it is bound to shrivel and to cut off its creative energies: at first it permits innovation only on the foundations of the old, then freedom is restricted to the freedom to interpret, after that it becomes permissible only to interpret the meaning of the interpretations, until finally all that is left is to polish the artifacts in their cases.

A living civilization is a perpetual drama of struggle between interpretations, outside influences, and emphases, an unrelenting struggle over what is wheat and what is the chaff. Rebellion for the sake of innovation. Dismantling for the purpose of reassembling differently. And even putting things in storage to clear the stage for experiment and for new creativity.

And it is permissible to seek inspiration from, and be fertilized by, other civilizations as well. This implies a realization that struggle and pluralism are not just an eclipse or a temporary aberration, but rather the natural climate for a living culture.

The heretic and the prober are sometimes the harbingers of the creator and the innovator. . . . Museum or drama, ritual or creativity, total orientation toward the past (what was is what will be), a world in which every question has an answer from the holy books, every new enemy is simply the reincarnation of an ancient one, every new situation is simply the reincarnation of an old and familiar one, or not? Can it be that history is not a spinning wheel but a twisting line, which even if it has loops and curves is essentially linear, not circular?

I must tell you that the rendezvous between a Jew like me and Western humanism, with its top roots in the European Renaissance and its tap root in earlier times, has no similarity to all the previous rendezvous between Judaism and Hellenism, or Judaism and Islamic culture. This rendezvous with Western humanism is a fateful one, formative, constitutional, irrevocable. And if you should ask, "why is this meeting different from all the other meetings?" I would tell you that when we, my forefathers and I, met up with European humanism during the last few cen turies, particularly in its liberal and socialist forms, perhaps we recognized in it, perhaps my forefathers recognized in it, certain astounding genetic similarities. Because Western humanism has Jewish genes as well.

Who is a Jew? Whoever is wrestling with the question "Who is a Jew?" Here is our personal definition: any human being crazy enough to call himself a Jew is a Jew. Is he or she a good or a bad Jew? This is up to the next Jew to say.

This book may not hold too many words, but it is populated by a great many Jews. We want to end it with a non-Jew: Jorge Luis Borges, a writer, a librarian, and a magus of language.

In his short story "Pierre Mcnard, Author of the *Quixote*," written in the dry terminology of a bibliographer, Borges tells how a (nonexistent) modern French novelist sits down one day and writes, in Spanish, word for word, Miguel de Cervantes' seventeenth-century classic, *Don Quixote*.

Pay close attention: Menard does not *translate*, or *copy*, or *quote*, or *paraphrase*, or *review*, or *comment upon*, Cervantes' book. He *authors* it. It is now a new book. It is Menard's book.

Every time we, or you, or the rabbi, or the rabbi's daughter, read a text, we author it in our own image. God's book becomes Isaiah's book, and Rabban Yohanan's book, and Osnat Barazani's book, and our book, and your book. Even if we repeat ancient words verbatim, they are no longer the ancient words, they are new now, and they are ours, in our image, in our contexts, until the next author comes along, the next Pierre Menard.

For you can never step into the same river twice, said the wise Greek philosopher Heraclitus. And his disciple Cratylus added: not even once.

Our words are not our words. They change as we utter them. They never stay long enough to "belong." A little like our offspring, in the already-quoted line of the wise Arab poet Gibran: Your children are not your children. We may wish our children to continue our words; instead, they will author the book afresh.

So it is with "the Jews." Often, in this essay and out there in the world, the Jews are not the Jews. They are all of mankind as it comes to grips with story, meaning, and law, laid down in writing. Try to replace the word *Jew* in this book with *reader*. In many places you'd be surprised how well it works.

Even anti-Semitism can at times translate into sheer brutal silencing, book burning, Web-blocking, and censorship. Everywhere.

Text and individuality, humor and argument, women with tongues and children with questions—are they not modes of all human existence, apparent in every human abode, if only allowed?

Yes, some things are untranslatable, thank heaven. Languages, for instance. The granite splendor of Hebrew and the coarse spice of Yiddish can never become universal flavors. And Grandma, too, let us leave her there on the beach, in all her ancestral Jewish grit, testing the Lord Almighty, grandson in arms.

But all other things Jewish are free-for-all, to anyone crazy enough to claim them.

sources

ONE

Continuity

This chapter's motto is from *Sepher Yetzirah*, the Book of Formation (or Creation), an esoteric Hebrew text probably written early in the first millennium CE, probably in Israel. The three components of all that exists, "Number, Writing, and Speech," are in Hebrew *sfar, sefer,* and *sipur,* all derived from the triliteral ספר. We have used the English translation by W. W. Wescott (1887) available on http://www.sacred-texts.com/jud/yetzirah.htm. Thanks to Rachel Elior for this reference.

Not a bloodline but a textline: our approach to Jewish continuity does not exclude the plurality of Jewish experiences or the ever-present fruitful interactions between Jewish and non-Jewish cultures, as recently and tellingly explored in *Cultures of the Jews: A New History*, ed. David Biale (New York: Schocken, 2002). However, we remain committed to a view of Jewish texts as primarily and constantly conversing with previous Jewish texts. For this emphasis on inner conversation over the ages see David Roskies's review of Biale's volume in *Commentary,* February 2003.

Such continuity has recently been disputed: see especially Shlomo

Sand, *The Invention of the Jewish People,* trans. Yael Lotan (London: Verso, 2008). While Sand rejects any biblical "origin" of present-day Jews, equating peoplehood with race-based nationality, other authors have attempted to demote biblical origins by arguing that many of the Bible's purported historical narratives are unsupported by archaeological facts on the ground. See especially Israel Finkelstein and Neil Asher Silberman, *The Bible Unearthed: Archaeology's New Vision of Ancient Israel and the Origin of Its Sacred Texts* (New York: Free Press, 2001). We find these books thoughtful and challenging, but strongly disagree with their respective understandings of Jewish continuity, what it is about, and what is really important therein.

Yehuda Amichai's poem "The Jews" was published in his book *Even a Fist Was Once an Open Palm with Fingers,* 1989. Here and in Chapter 4 we give our own translation, but see Barbara and Benjamin Harshav's English rendering (New York: HarperCollins, 1991).

Yizhar Smilansky's "The Courage to Be Secular: The Religious, the Non-Religious, and the Secular" was published in Hebrew in *Shdemot* 79 (1981). English translation by Shmuel Gertel, to appear in *New Jewish Culture: New Jewish Thought in Israel,* ed. Yaakov Malkin, forthcoming.

Do Modern Hebrew speakers "understand" biblical Hebrew? Ghil'ad Zuckermann recently disputed Modern Hebrew's claim even to be called "Hebrew" at all, proposing to regard it as "Israeli," a latter-day hybrid of Ancient Hebrew, Yiddish, and other languages: Zuckermann, *Israelit Safa Yafa* (Israeli: A beautiful language) (Tel Aviv: Am Oved, 2008). We respectfully disagree.

Three words, all nouns, brimming with meaning: see Erich Auerbach's account of biblical conciseness, contrasted with ancient Greek's epic long-windedness, in the wonderful first chapter, "Odysseus' Scar," of his book *Mimesis: The Representation of Reality in Western Literature,* first published in 1946, trans. Willard Trask (Princeton: Princeton University Press, 2003).

The Talmud as an ancient Hebrew text: although much of the Talmud is in Aramaic, we still call it a Hebrew text, by merit of its constant engagement with biblical content and by virtue of the first-cousinhood of Hebrew and Aramaic.

Mordecai Kaplan on Jewish civilization: *Judaism as a Civilization: Toward a Reconstruction of American-Jewish Life* (1934; Philadelphia: Jewish Publication Society, 2010), 196.

"And Moses received the Torah from Sinai"—Mishnah, Avot, chapter 1.

Exactly who were the Elders? Cf. Michael Walzer, "Biblical Politics: Where Were the Elders?" *Hebraic Political Studies* 3:3 (2008), 225.

"Hillel the Elder had eighty disciples": Babylonian Talmud, Baba Bathra 134a.

The tale of Elisha ben Abuya on horseback, his conversation with Rabbi Meir, and the latter's successful efforts, together with Rabbi Yohanan, to secure *Acher*'s eternal rest is told in the Babylonian Talmud, Hagigah 15a and 15b.

The tale of Akhnai's Oven, also known as "Not in Heaven": Babylonian Talmud, Baba Mezi'a 59b.

Menachem Brinker's observation on Akhnai's Oven was made in a letter to the authors.

"They said of Rabban Yohanan ben Zakai": Babylonian Talmud, Sukkah 28a.

Woody Allen's roller coaster reader: "A Little Louder, Please," *New Yorker*, May 28, 1966.

"When he sat and occupied himself with the Torah": ibid.

"A person is jealous of everyone, except his son and his disciple": Babylonian Talmud, Sanhedrin 104b.

"Generation to generation": This phrasing is in Psalms 145. More prevalent in the Bible is the phrase "in each generation and generation."

"Suffer little children": Luke 18:16 and Matthew 19:14.

"A wise son makes his father glad": Proverbs 10:1. Variations can be found in Proverbs 13:1 and 15:20.

On Glikl of Hameln and her reading see Natalie Zemon Davis, *Women on the Margins: Three Seventeenth-Century Lives* (Cambridge: Harvard University Press, 1995), chapter 1, especially 22–24.

No *sancta simplicitas* for the Jews: Many centuries later, some Hasidic tales conveyed an enchantment with the Dumb Youth beloved by God. This never did, and never could, become a pedagogic model.

"If your son asks you tomorrow": Exodus 13:14.

Venturing deeper into the orchard: the famous tale of four scholars who "entered the orchard" of profound learning, of whom only one emerged unscathed, is told in the Tosefta, Seder Moed, Hagigah 2:2; and in the Jerusalem Talmud, Seder Moed, Hagigah 9a.

Father-and-daughter interlocutors in the history of Jewish learning: Shmuel and Osnat Barazani, Rashi and his three daughters, and Moses and Dorothea Mendelssohn spring to mind. Mothers conducted intergenerational conversations too: Glikl of Hameln is a shining example.

Early modern books for women: Jacob Ashkenazi's *Tzena urena* of 1616 is the best-known example, but some biblical texts can be seen as predecessors, including "The Woman of Valor" in Proverbs 31, and possibly, in a rather different way, the Song of Songs; we shall later return to them.

Freud on Jewish neurosis: Quoted by Sander L. Gilman, *Freud, Race, and Gender* (Princeton: Princeton University Press, 1993), 110.

Jewish traits becoming emblems of universal modernity: for a masterly perusal of this theme see Yuri Slezkine, *The Jewish Century* (Princeton: Princeton University Press, 2004).

Jews talk a lot: Verbs denoting "speak," "say," or "talk" appear in the Bible more than six thousand times, making the utterance of words its most common type of activity. By comparison, the verb for "do" or "make" has fewer than two thousand appearances.

In a fascinating conversation, Susannah Heschel suggested to the historian among us that Shylock's monologue (*Merchant of Venice*, act III, scene i) was designed to arouse contempt in Shakespeare's audience, due to the vulgar corporeal nature of the Jew's claims. This may well have been the case, but Shylock's quintessentially Jewish disputativeness, stubborn, eloquent, and against all odds, still shines through the allegedly anti-Semitic ridicule.

"Inside each Jew there were so many speakers!": Philip Roth, *Operation Shylock* (New York: Simon and Schuster, 1993), 335. Cf. Josh Cohen, "Roth's Doubles," in *The Cambridge Companion to Philip*

Roth, ed. Timothy Parris (Cambridge: Cambridge University Press 2007), 85.

"The past is a foreign country": L. P. Hartley, *The Go-Between* (London: H. Hamilton, 1953), 1; David Lowenthal, *The Past Is a Foreign Country* (Cambridge: Cambridge University Press, 1985).

TWO
Vocal Women

"Ashir li-Shlomo," ascribing the Song of Songs to a female voice: S. D. Goitein, "The Song of Songs: A Female Composition," in *A Feminist Companion to the Song of Songs,* ed. Athalya Brenner (Sheffield: Sheffield Academic Press, 1993), 58–66. Goitein quoted Yaakov Nahum Epstein as an earlier exponent of the same idea. Another possible predecessor is the German pastor G. Kuhn, *Erklärung des Hohen Liedes* (Leipzig: Deichert, 1926).

"It is uncouth for a woman always to leave home" is from Maimonides, *Mishneh Torah,* chapter 13, Halakha 11.

The Bible is teeming with outgoing, vociferous women—see, among other places, Exodus 15:20–21, Judges 5:1, 1 Samuel 2:1–10, 1 Samuel 18:6–7, and 1 Chronicles 25:5–6. Some scholars now doubt whether the word *machol,* associated with Miriam and the women of Israel in our Exodus quotation, indeed meant "dance," and suggest that it denoted a musical instrument. This alternative does not seem to detract from the sense of outdoor female merrymaking. In numerous biblical accounts of public festivity, women are linked with *machol.* See also Jeremiah 31:3 and 12.

"Men-singers and women-singers" appear in 2 Samuel 19:36, Ecclesiastes 2:8, Ezra 2:65, and Nehemiah 7:67.

Old Barzillai can no longer hear women's singing in 2 Samuel 19:36.

The Altschulers' commentaries, *Metzudat David* and its counterpart *Metzudat Zion,* were printed in Livorno in 1780–82. "Male and Female to sing on the road" pertains to Nehemiah 7:67. See also JewishEncyclopedia.com under "Altschul."

"David According to Dita" is from Amos Oz, *The Same Sea*, trans. Nicholas de Lange in collaboration with the author (London: Chatto and Windus, 2001).

The Talmudic tale of David, Avishag, and Bathsheba is in the Babylonian Talmud, Sanhedrin 22a.

On Michal see 1 Samuel 18:20–28 and 19:11–17, 2 Samuel 6:20–23. On Abigail see 1 Samuel 25:2–42. On Bathsheba see 2 Samuel 11:2–27 and 12:1–25, 1 Kings 1:11–31 and 2:13–22, and she even gets a sneak mention in Psalms 51:2. Don't let this long list of citations put you off. The stories are delicious. There's sex, but it is counterbalanced, as it should be, with political intrigue, family drama, and a good range of human emotions.

The story of David, Michal, and dirty dancing in front of the Ark of the Covenant is in 2 Samuel 6:20–23. It may seem cruel, and certainly un-Jewish, that God punished Michal with childlessness. The Bible itself seems ambivalent about this: in 2 Samuel 21:8, Michal is on record with no fewer than five sons, though not by David. Want to know how the Mishnaic sages explained away this discrepancy? Check the Tosefta, Sotah, 11:9.

"No women were found so beautiful as the daughters of Job"— Job 42:15.

"The wind wrote them on her dress"—Divrei Iyov 48:1–3, quoted by Rachel Elior, "Alternative Haggadah: Four Daughters Worth Mentioning at Pesach," *Haaretz,* April 7, 2009, http://www.haaretz.com/alternative-haggadah-four-daughters-worth-mentioning-at-pesach-1.273731.

Plato tells of Socrates' mother, Phaenarete, in his dialogue *Theaetetus*.

Deborah, Jael, and Sisera play out their bloody drama in Judges 4. Athalia, Jehosheba, and baby Joash are in 2 Kings 11:1–2.

Miriam, Deborah, and Hannah sing their songs of praise in Exodus 15:20–21, Judges 5, and 1 Samuel 2:1–10, respectively.

Tamar's story is in Genesis 38.

The earlier Deborah, Rebecca's wet nurse, makes her quick peek from obscurity in Genesis 35:8. There, she dies and is buried in Beth El. But even though she was only a wet nurse, the Bible saw fit to give us her name, mention her claim to our memory, and tell us of the oak tree under which she was buried, and of the name of the tree, given on that occasion perhaps by Jacob himself, "the Oak of Mourning." In one verse, relating her death, the Bible resurrects that humble woman for us, names and entitles and honors her.

For a different take on biblical versus ancient Greek female protagonists, see Matthew B. Schwartz and Kalman J. Kaplan, *The Fruit of Her Hands: A Psychology of Biblical Woman* (Grand Rapids, Mich.: Eerdmans, 2007), chapter 1.

The terrible story of the mother and her seven sons, which we deem atypical, is nevertheless repeated and eulogized in many Jewish sources, among them 2 Maccabees 7, 4 Maccabees, and the Babylonian Talmud, Gittin 57:72. The name Hannah appears in some later sources.

Itzik Manger's overloving mother is in the poem *Oyfn Veg Shteyt a Boym* (On the road stands a tree), probably written in the 1930s. With the beautiful and heartbreaking tune, ascribed to P. Laskovsky and possibly based on Romanian folk music, it became an emblematic Yiddish song. You can find it on YouTube in Hebrew and English versions, something of a vocal tombstone to Yiddish culture. But an irony lurks therein: Manger's source and inspiration was an early Zionist song, sung by the nineteenth-century eastern European pioneers of *chibbat zion,* and their tree stands on the road to the Land of Israel. Relationships between Yiddishism and Zionism have frequently been strained and estranged, even today, both in academic and in ultra-Orthodox circles. *Oyfn Veg Shteyt a Boym* is a gentle reminder of the complicated mother-and-son connection between Yiddish culture and modern Israel's founders.

Hannah brings Samuel to Shiloh with food and wine, and visits him annually with a new little coat, in 1 Samuel 1:24 and 2:19. Elkanah is attentive to his wife, within limits but still rather impressively, in 1 Samuel 1:8.

Ruth's words to Naomi, "Whither thou goest," can be read in Ruth 1:16.

The Woman of Valor, who "openeth her mouth with wisdom," is in Proverbs 31:10–31.

Hulda the Prophetess speaks in 2 Kings 22:14 and in 2 Chronicles 34:22. The Wise Woman of Tekoa is in 2 Samuel 14. The Divining Woman of En-Dor is in 1 Samuel 28. The Big Woman of Shunem is in 2 Kings 4:8–37.

Bertolt Brecht's lines "So many reports. / So many questions" are from his poem "Questions of a Worker Who Reads," originally titled "Fragen eines lesenden Arbeiters" (1935), in: Bertolt Brecht, *Poems, 1913–1956*, trans. M. Hamburger (New York: Methuen, 1976). It begins: "Who built Thebes of the seven gates? / In the books you will find the name of kings. / Did the kings haul up the lumps of rock?"

Ecclesiastes claims to "find the woman more bitter than death," and the rest of it, in 7:26, 28. This book is superb, regardless.

Rabbi Akiva and his wife: the story is gleaned from several sources. See Babylonian Talmud, Ketubbot 62b and Nedarim 50a; Jerusalem Talmud, Shabbat 34a; and Avot d'Rabbi Nathan, version A, chapter 6; version B, chapter 12. The latter names her Rachel.

The unnamed *tannaim,* along with Rabbi Eliezer and Rabbi Eleazar, wax misogynist in the Mishnah, Avot 1:5; ibid., Sotah 3:4; and Jerusalem Talmud, Sotah 3, respectively.

Josephus Flavius's questionable quote from the Torah is in *Contra Apionem* (circa 96–100 CE), 2:25.

Ben Azzai's claim that "a man must teach his daughter Torah" is contradicted by Rabbi Eliezer in the Mishnah, Avot 1:5. "God gave women more understanding than men" is in the Babylonian Talmud, Niddah 45b.

"And you shall tell your son," or "your children," comes from Exodus 13:8.

The modest mother of sages Kimchit is in the Jerusalem Talmud, Yoma 5a, Megilla 14a, and Horayot 16b, and in the Babylonian Talmud, Yoma 47a.

Ima Shalom on the Gates of Hurt Feelings: Babylonian Talmud, Baba Mezi'a 59b.

The precocious Yalta made clever remarks and performed memorable deeds in the Babylonian Talmud, Hulin 109a, Brachot 51b, Beitza 25b, and Gittin 67b.

As for Bruria, see Babylonian Talmud, Brachot 10a and Eiruvin

53b–54a, where the Lod anecdote appears. "Well Said Bruria" is from Tosefta, Kelim, Baba Mezi'a 1:3.

"Ten measures of speech descended to the world," according to the Babylonian Talmud, Kidushin 49b.

Rachel Elior discusses Jewish women's discrimination in her essay "Like Sophia and Marcelle and Lizzie," in *Dybbuks and Jewish Women in Social History, Mysticism, and Folklore* (New York: Urim, 2008).

On the rising status and literacy of Jewish women in various diasporas during the Middle Ages see especially Avraham Grossman, *Pious and Rebellious: Jewish Women in Medieval Europe,* trans. Jonathan Chipman (Waltham, Mass.: Brandeis University Press, 2004), chapters 7–8 and 13.

"Will her love remember his graceful doe"—for the poem's English translation, see *The Dream of the Poem: Hebrew Poetry from Muslim and Christian Spain, 950–1492,* trans. and ed. Peter Cole (Princeton: Princeton University Press, 2007), 27, 263–65; for its unique story, see Adina Hoffman and Peter Cole, *Sacred Trash: The Lost and Found World of the Cairo Geniza* (New York: Schocken, 2011), 179 and passim. Ezra Fleischer presented his hypothesis on Dunash's wife as the author in his article "On Dunash Ben Labrat, His Wife and Son" *Mechkarei Yerushalaim beSifrut Ivrit* 5 (1984), 189–202.

Rashi's daughters: alongside Maggie Anton's eponymous trilogy of historical novels, see her article "Rashi and His Daughters," *Judaism: A Quarterly Journal of Jewish Life and Thought,* January 2005.

Data on Jewish women's literacy is scarce for the Middle Ages, better but still largely anecdotal for the early modern era, and increasingly solid from the late eighteenth century onward. We have benefited from fascinating recent studies touching on female erudition by Rachel Elior, Elisheva Baumgarten, Avraham Grossman, Howard Tzvi Adelman, Natalie Zemon Davis, Deborah Hertz, and Iris Parush. This list is by no means comprehensive.

Iris Parush maps and analyzes the great rise of female literacy in the era of the Jewish Enlightenment, the Haskalah, in *Reading Jewish Women: Marginality and Modernization in Nineteenth-Century Eastern European Jewish Society,* trans. Saadya Sternberg (Waltham, Mass.: Brandeis University Press, 2004).

Isaac Bashevis Singer's *In My Father's Court* (New York: Farrar, Straus and Giroux, 1966) provides many telling illustrations of our subject matter. For the anecdotes mentioned here see pages 19, 44, and 141.

Chief Justice Haim Cohn tells of his rabbinical grandmother in his beautiful autobiography *Mavo ishi: otobiografia* (Or Yehuda: Kinneret, Zmora Bitan, Dvir, 2005), 82–85.

On Joseph Klausner and his female peers in Heidelberg see Fania Oz-Salzberger's festive lecture of 2003, "Heidelberg's Hope," http://www.uni-heidelberg.de/press/news/2310salz.html.

THREE
Time and Timelessness

Tehom, after its impressive first mention in Genesis 1:2, appears three more times in Genesis, and also in Isaiah, Ezekiel, Amos, Jonah, Habakkuk, Psalms, Job, and Proverbs. In many of these places God is "over" or "above" Tehom. The great sea monsters, in Hebrew *Taninim,* are singled out among all other living creatures in Genesis 1:21. Isaiah and Psalms sing God's praises as victor over them, and poor Job complains, "Am I a sea, or a sea monster, that Thou settest a watch over me?" (Job 7:12). Similarly, God hunts and kills Leviathan, or at least plays with him, in Isaiah, Psalms, and Job.

Bashevis Singer looks for Leviathan in the Vistula: *In My Father's Court,* 179.

Modern scholars dug up these mythical relics like rare fossils from the Bible's monotheistic soil. See especially Yehezkel Kaufmann, *The Religion of Israel: From Its Beginning to the Babylonian Exile,* trans. and abridged, Moshe Greenberg (Chicago: University of Chicago Press, 1960); Umberto Cassuto, *The Goddess Anath: Canaanite Epics on the Patriarchal Age,* trans. Israel Abrahams (Jerusalem: Hebrew University Magnes Press, 1971). The historian among us affectionately recalls a good high school teacher, Uri Lazovsky, who introduced her into the magical world of prebiblical monsters and post-Orthodox exegesis.

"A people that shall dwell alone" is in Numbers 23:9. In fairness to Balaam, the words are purportedly God's, put in his mouth. Besides, there are differing interpretations for what the word *yitchashav*, here translated as "reckoned," might mean.

The day that shall be "neither day nor night" appears in Zechariah 14:7–8. It is quoted in an enigmatic, nocturnal *piyut* (Jewish liturgical poem) titled "Karev Yom," by the poet Yannai, in the Land of Israel in the sixth century CE. Then it became part of the Haggadah. The historian among us was surely not the only Jewish child terrified and bewitched by it at the close of the Passover Seder. To hear modern renderings of this and many other *piyutim*, simply go to the admirable http://www.piyut.org.il/english/.

"That which hath been is that which shall be" is in Ecclesiastes 1:9.

The Bible has more holy times than holy places: we owe this insight to Rachel Elior.

"It does make sense to speak of the future": Jurek Becker, *Jakob the Liar,* originally published in 1969, trans. Leila Vennewitz (London: Plume, 1999), 40.

Rachel Elior compared literary evidence with archaeological evidence in a letter to the authors.

Naomi Shemer is quoted on the Bible, "This fable is more alive than all the stones," in Dalia Karpel, "Ein la-zeh mashma'ut" (It has no meaning), *Haaretz,* October 29, 1999.

On "the end of days" see Isaiah 2:2 and Micah 4:1. Daniel too has "the end of days," 10:14, and "the end of wonders," 12:6. Ezekiel 38:8 speaks of "the end of years." In most of these places the future of specific nations is discussed, rather than individuals or mankind as a whole. We rest our case: where there are nations, there is politics and there is history.

Jacob's "end of days" speech starts in Genesis 49:1.

"Every man under his vine and under his fig-tree" appears, with small variations, in 1 Kings 5:5, 2 Kings 18:31, Isaiah 36:16, and Micah 4:4.

Leviathan and Wild Ox are on the Jewish afterlife menu from the Babylonian Talmud, Baba Bathra 75a, through many subsequent sources and versions, most recently in Haim Be'er's novel *El makom she-haruch holech* (the English title is *Back from Heavenly Lack,* and we hope an English translation will ensue) (Jerusalem: Am Oved, 2011), where a great ultra-Orthodox rabbi, bottomless textual memory, modern science, Tibetan politics, and a Wild Ox play intricate Midrashic games.

Isaac Leib Peretz's story *Sholem Bayis* (Domestic bliss) can be read in English translation, titled "Domestic Happiness," in Isaac Leib Peretz, *Stories and Pictures,* trans. Helena Frank (1906, rpt. Ann Arbor: University of Michigan Library, 2009), 21–28. Here we offer our own translation from the Hebrew.

Adin Steinsaltz on the Hebrew syntax of time is quoted, and the idea expanded, by Shulamith Hareven, "Language as Midrash," in her book *Mashiah o knesset* (Tel Aviv: Zmora Bitan, 1987).

"The backside of a lion"—Rabban Yohanan in the Babylonian Talmud, Berachot 61a.

"A garden eastward in Eden"—Genesis 2:8. Cain "dwelt in land of Nod, on the east of Eden"—Genesis 4:16.

Naphtali Herz Imber authored *Hatikvah* as *Tikvatenu* in 1878.

"There is no early or late in the Torah"—Jerusalem Talmud, Shekalim 25b and Sotah 37a; Babylonian Talmud, Pesachim 6b.

Nahmanides' objection is in his exegesis to Numbers 9:1 and 15:1.

Baruch Spinoza broke new ground in biblical criticism in his *Tractatus Theologico-Politicus* (Amsterdam, 1670): "I determined to examine the Bible afresh in a careful, impartial, and unfettered spirit, making no assumptions concerning it, and attributing to it no doctrines, which I do not find clearly therein set down," he wrote in the preface. Trans. Robert Harvey Monro Elwes (London: George Bell and Sons, 1891).

"When was Job?"—Jerusalem Talmud, Sotah 25b; Babylonian Talmud, Nezikin 15a.

"Down into the garden of nuts"—Song of Songs 6:11.

"Four went in the orchard"—Tosefta, Hagigah B2; Jerusalem Talmud, Moed 9a.

On Nahmanides, Moses de Léon, the Holy Ari, and the four-stage exegetic model of *peshat, remez, drash,* and *sod* see Gershom Scholem, *Major Trends in Jewish Mysticism* (1941; New York: Schocken, 1995), including the foreword by Robert Alter; Amos Funkenstein, *Perceptions of Jewish History* (Berkeley: University of California Press, 1995).

The timeless tale of God, Moses, and Akiva is in the Babylonian Talmud, Menachoth 29b. The original is in Aramaic. For a recent English translation and discussion, see Christine Hayes, *The Emergence of Judaism: Classical Traditions in Contemporary Perspective* (Minneapolis: Fortress, 2010), 107–8.

God's answer to Job is from Job 38:4–5 and 16–18.

Shmuel Yosef Agnon, "Two Scholars Who Lived in Our Town," is included in the sixth volume of his collected writings, *Samukh venir'eh* (Jerusalem: Schocken, 1979), 5–53. The title harks back to the Babylonian Talmud, Sotah 49a.

The story of Moses, God, and Eliezer is from Midrash Tanhuma, Chukot 8. Thanks again to Haim Be'er.

Mordecai Kaplan on Judaism's "monopoly on the first years of the child's upbringing": *Judaism as a Civilization: Toward a Reconstruction of American-Jewish Life* (1934; rpt. Philadelphia: Jewish Publication Society, 2010), 196.

Our tiny sample of biblical protagonists in modern Hebrew literature includes Abraham Mapu, *The Love of Zion,* trans. Joseph Marymount (1853; Jerusalem: Toby, 2006); A. B. Yehoshua, *A Journey to the End of the Millennium,* trans. Nicholas de Lange (New York: Doubleday, 1999); and Zeruya Shalev, *Love Life: A Novel,* trans. Dalya Bilu (New York: Grove, 2001).

Heine speaks of Shylock, Jessica, and the affinity of Jews and Germans in his essay "Shylock" (1838), in: Heinrich Heine, *Jewish Stories and Hebrew Melodies,* trans. Frederic Ewen (Princeton: Markus Wiener, 1987). See especially p. 90.

On the tragedy of the German Jews see especially two remarkable works: Frederic V. Grunfeld, *Prophets Without Honor: Background to Freud, Kafka, Einstein, and Their World* (London: Hutchinson, 1979); and Amos Elon, *The Pity of It All: A Portrait of the German-Jewish Epoch, 1743–1933* (New York: Picador, 2002).

In 1942, the great poet and political columnist Nathan Alterman wrote his own "Lorelei," bitterly paraphrasing some of Heine's celebrated lines: "And the city burnt books, and the fires flickered / As Lorelei danced on a casket of liquor / . . . She threw into the pyre [Heine's] Buch der Lieder / . . . And driving past Heine, Miss Lorelei / Aimed, and shot, and he fell to the wall. / The poet is mortal; everlasting the poem" (our translation). Nathan Alterman, *Hatur hashvi'i* (The seventh column), vol. 1 (Tel Aviv: Hakibbutz hameuchad, 1948).

Maimonides on the "enslavement by kingdoms"—quoted from the Babylonian Talmud, Berachot 34b.

On the importance of Samson in modern Hebrew/Israeli culture see David Fishelov, *Machlefot Shimshon (Samson's Locks): The Transformations of Biblical Samson* (Haifa and Tel Aviv: Haifa University Press and Zmora Bitan, 2000).

On Abba Kovner see Dina Porat, *The Fall of a Sparrow: The Life and Times of Abba Kovner*, trans. and ed. Elizabeth Yuval (Palo Alto: Stanford University Press, 2009).

Lambs to the slaughter: Isaiah 43:7, Jeremiah 12:3, Psalms 44:23, and the Book of Yossifon, Italy, tenth century CE.

Simha Luzzatto's *Discourse on the Jews of Venice* (1638)—the passage quoted here is our English translation from the Hebrew edition, *Ma'amar al yehudei Venezia*, trans. D. Lattes (Jerusalem: Mossad Bialik, 1951), 122–23, quoted by Haim Hillel Ben-Sasson, *Toldot am yisrael bi-yemey habeinayim* (Ganei Aviv: Dvir, 2002), 289. We are grateful to Yosef Kaplan for this reference, and for his sharp eye for the modern kernels in early modern Jewish thinkers.

On Luzzatto's two audiences see Ariella Lang, "The Double Edge of Irony in Simone Luzzatto's *Discorso*," *Jewish Social Studies* 15:3 (2009), 114–33.

"Planet Auschwitz" and its different time sphere: Ka-Tzetnik 135633, *Shivitti: A Vision,* 2nd ed., trans. Eliyah Nike De-Nur and Lisa Herman (Nevada City, Calif.: Gateways, 1998), xvii.

Dan Pagis, "Katuv be-iparon ba-karon ha'chatum" (Written in pencil in the sealed wagon), *Gilgul* (Tel Aviv: Masada, 1970). The English translation is ours.

FOUR

Each Person Has a Name

"Three names by which a person is called": Midrash Tanhuma, va-yakhel 1.

For Amichai's poem "The Jews" see notes to Chapter 1. The translation, again, is our own.

"Blessed is the Creator of all manner of perfumes"—Babylonian Talmud, Blessings 43a–b.

Yosef Haim Brenner, "There is no Judaism outside our own selves," from *Kol Kitvei Y. H. Brenner,* vol. 2 (Tel Aviv: Hakkibutz Hameuchad, 1960), quoted by Gideon Shimoni, "Ideological Perspectives," in *Zionism in Transition,* ed. Moshe Davis (New York: Arno, 1980), 20.

Micah Yosef Berdyczewski's "Jews have seniority over Judaism" is in his collected essays, *Kol Ma'amarei Micha Yosef Ben Gurion* (Tel Aviv: Am Oved, 1952), 30.

Saadia Gaon wrote that "the nation is only a nation by virtue of its Torahs" in *The Book of Beliefs and Opinions,* trans. Samuel Rosenblatt (New Haven: Yale University Press, 1948), 158. Cf. Alan Mittelman, "Judaism: Covenant, Pluralism, and Piety," in *The New Blackwell Companion to the Sociology of Religion,* ed. Bryan S. Turner (Oxford: Wiley-Blackwell, 2010), 340.

Berdyczewski's phrase, "We were a people and thought so and so, but we were not a people because we thought so and so," is quoted in Menachem Brinker, *Machshavot yisraeliot* (Israeli thoughts) (Jerusalem: Carmel, 2007), 41. We thank Professor Brinker for further elucidation.

For Hasidic stories, including tales of "hidden righteous men," leaf through Martin Buber's classic *Tales of the Hasidim* (1947); new ed. introduced by Chaim Potok (New York: Schocken, 1991). On Hasidic mysticism and egalitarianism see Rachel Elior, *The Mystical Origins of Hasidism* (Oxford: Littman Library of Jewish Civilization, 2006).

Ha'entziklopedia ha'ivrit, the *Hebrew Encyclopedia,* was a great feat of academic publishing, incorporating articles by some of the best scholars of the young State of Israel. Dreamed up in 1944—an astounding and heartbreaking timing—its thirty-two main volumes were published between 1948 and 1980. Its editors and contributors included Joseph Klausner, Ben-Zion Netanyahu, Nathan Rothenstreich, Yeshayahu Leibowitz, and Yehoshua Prawer. New volumes were edited by Nathan Shaham in the 1990s, and a new edition is currently under construction with, we hope, an online version. The project's visionary publishers were Bracha Peli and her son Alexander Peli. The encyclopedia was stamped by its creators' Jewish, universalist, and humanist worldview. Its subtitle is *General, Jewish, and Israeli* [*eretz-yisraelit*].

The renaming of Jacob at Yabbok, "For thou hast striven with God and with men, and hast prevailed," is in Genesis 32:29.

John Bunyan is quoted from his *Solomon's Temple Spiritualized* (1688; rpt. Minneapolis: Curiosmith, 2010), 77.

The Zelophehad sisters are in Numbers 27. See also Numbers 26:33 and 2 Chronicles 7:15. They "stood before Moses" in Numbers 27:2.

Early modern political philosophers who read a republican theory into ancient Israel: see Lea Campos Boralevi, "Classical Foundational Myths of European Republicanism: The Jewish Commonwealth," in *Republicanism: A Shared European Heritage,* vol. 1, *Republicanism and Constitutionalism in Early Modern Europe,* ed. Martin van Gelderen and Quentin Skinner (Cambridge: Cambridge University Press, 2002); Fania Oz-Salzberger, "The Jewish Roots of the Modern Republic," *Azure* 13 (2002), 88–132; Eric Nelson, *The Hebrew Republic: Jewish Sources and the Transformation of European Political Thought* (Cambridge: Harvard University Press, 2010).

On John Selden see Jason Rappaport, *Renaissance England's Chief Rabbi: John Selden* (Oxford: Oxford University Press, 2006).

Moses rules on the Zelophehad case in Numbers 27:6–9. "Let them be married to whom they think best" is in Numbers 36:6–7.

Milton's "dead Judaisms" are in his essay "The Reason of Church Government," book 2, chapter 3. See John Milton, *A Complete Collection of the Historical, Political, and Miscellaneous Works* (Amsterdam, 1698), 231. Available online.

On Judaizing and Judaizers in early modern England see David

Katz, *Philo-Semitism and the Readmission of the Jews to England 1603–1655* (Oxford: Clarendon, 1982).

The verse from Maccabees is from book 2, chapter 2:21.

Zechariah's futuristic Jew is in Zechariah (naturally), 8:23.

If you read Hebrew, look up the Academy for the Hebrew Language at hebrew-academy.huji.ac.il/, as well as the refreshing www.safa-ivrit.org, for many more fascinating data on the language's history, interlinguistic relations, and reawakening.

Bellow reminisced on his conversation with Agnon in a talk given in 1988 and published as "A Jewish Writer in America," part 1, *New York Review of Books,* October 27, 2011.

The Qur'an has the "People of the Book" in Surat Al-Baqarah 2:101, 2:105, and passim; Surat Āli 'Imrān 3:19, 3:20, and passim.

Emma Lazarus's English: the author of "Songs of a Semite" and "An Epistle to the Hebrews," who was nevertheless skeptical about synagogue worship and preserving the Hebrew language, is certainly a link in our textline. Cf. Michael P. Kramer, "Beginnings and Ends: The Origins of Jewish American Literary History," in *The Cambridge Companion to Jewish American Literature,* ed. Michael P. Kramer and Hana Wirth-Nesher (Cambridge: Cambridge University Press, 2003), 25–28.

"Whoever saves one soul" is in the Mishnah, Sanhedrin 4:5. The rephrasing into "soul of Israel" is in the Babylonian Talmud, Sanhedrin 37a. Maimonides leaves Israel out of it in *Mishneh Torah,* Hilchot Sanhedrin 7.

"For the blood is the soul (*nefesh*)," Deuteronomy 12:23.

Rabbi Jose subjects even the Sabbath to *pikuach nefesh* in Tosefta, Shabbat 16:13. The Babylonian Talmud distinguishes between saving Jews and non-Jews on the Sabbath in Yoma 84b. The rabbis debate in detail several hypothetic groups of persons needing to be rescued on the Sabbath: nine Jews and one foreigner, as against nine foreigners and one Jew. Not the Talmud's finest hour.

"Choose life" is from Deuteronomy 30:19.

"The light is sweet, and pleasant it is for the eyes to behold the sun" in Ecclesiastes 11:7.

Man "mints many coins in one mold" and God "stamped each

person with the seal of Adam" in the Mishnah, Sanhedrin 4:5. The wicked ask, "What does this trouble have to do with us?" in the same passage.

"These were the elect of the congregation"—Numbers 1:16–17.

"And the Lord spoke unto Moses" about future land distribution in Numbers 26:53–54.

Josephus Flavius called ancient Israel a "theocratic republic" in *The Antiquities of the Jews*, xiv.3.2.

"Make their Torah their art"—this harks back to the Babylonian Talmud, Berachot 15b, but many other places in the Talmud suggest that the rabbis wanted people to study the Torah alongside, not instead of, plying their trades.

Differing counts of the Amoraim are summed in Heshey Zelcer, *A Guide to the Jerusalem Talmud* (Boca Raton, Fla.: Universal, 2002), 56, note 63.

Zelda's poem "Le-khol ish yesh shem" was published in her book *Al tirkhak* (Tel Aviv: Hakkibutz Hameuchad, 1974). Put to music by Hanan Yovel, it is one of Israel's best-loved songs. For a different take on this poem and the naming motif in the context of Jewish secularity see Yedidya Itzhaki, *The Uncovered Head: Jewish Culture, New Perspectives* (Lanham, Md.: University of Delaware Press, 2011), chapter 1.

Epilogue

Khalil Gibran's "Your children are not your children"—"On Children," *The Prophet* (1923; New York: Knopf, 1995), 18.

Abraham and God argue in Genesis 18; Job and God begin in Job 3 and end in Job 42.

The King Solomon and the Old Rabbi jokes come from Alter Druyanov's invaluable *Sefer ha-bedicha veha-chidud* (The book of joke and witticism), first published in Frankfurt am Main: Omanut, 1922. We used the edition (Tel Aviv: Dvir, 1963) made available by the Ben-Yehuda Project, http://benyehuda.org/droyanov/.

On Judeo-Hispanic humor: Alegria Bendelac, "Humor and Affectivity in Jaquetia, the Judeo-Spanish Language of Northern Morocco," *Humor* 1–2 (1988), 177–86.

Ivan Karamazov hallucinates on the Grand Inquisitor and Christ in Fyodor Dostoevsky, *The Brothers Karamazov* (1879–80), book 5, chapter 5. There are no fewer than four Hebrew translations, the most recent and brilliant by Nily Mirsky (Tel Aviv: Am Oved, 2011).

Abraham's resounding reproach against God's justice is in Genesis 18:25.

Judaism is a civilization: Amos Oz, *In the Land of Israel,* trans. Maurie Goldberg-Bartura (New York: Harcourt, 1983), 135–38.

Jorge Luis Borges chimes our final note with "Pierre Menard, Author of the *Quixote*." It first appeared in the Argentinian journal *Sur* in May 1939, which happens to be the very month and year the author among us was born. English translation by James E. Irby is available at http://www.coldbacon.com/writing/borges-quixote.html. Lovers of Borges will not be surprised to learn that he translates into Hebrew extremely well.

Heraclitus, Cratylus, and the river: Plato, *Cratylus* 402a; Aristotle, *Metaphysics* 1010a13.

index